RENEWALS 691-4574

DATE DUE

CULTIVATING CRISIS

D1009735

WITHDRAWN
UTSA LIBRARIES

DOUGLAS L. MURRAY

Cultivating Crisis

The Human Cost of Pesticides in Latin America

University of Texas Press ◄►◄ Austin

Copyright © 1994 by the University of Texas Press
All rights reserved
Printed in the United States of America
First Edition, 1994

The excerpt from the poem "Lights" by Ernesto Cardenal, on pages 8 and 9, is from *Zero Hour and Other Documentary Poems* and is reprinted by permission of New Directions Publishing. The photographs on pages ii, 7, 55, 73, and 117 are by Donald Cole; the photograph on page 135 is by Peter Rosset; other photographs are by the author.

Requests for permission to reproduce material from this work should be sent to Permissions, University of Texas Press, Box 7819, Austin, TX 78713-7819.

∞ The paper used in this publication meets the minimum requirements of American National Standard for Information Sciences—Permanence of Paper for Printed Library Materials, ANSI Z39.48-1984.

Library of Congress Cataloging-in-Publication Data

Murray, Douglas L., date
    Cultivating crisis : the human cost of pesticides in Latin America / Douglas L. Murray. — 1st ed.
      p.   cm.
    Includes bibliographical references and index.
    ISBN 0-292-75168-0. — ISBN 0-292-75169-9 (pbk.)
    1. Pesticides—Latin America. 2. Pesticides—Toxicology—Latin America. 3. Pesticides—Environmental aspects—Latin America. 4. Cotton—Diseases and pests—Control—Latin America. 5. Agricultural pests—Control—Latin America. 6. Agriculture—Social aspects—Latin America. 7. Pesticides—Economic aspects—Latin America. 8. Produce trade—Latin America. 9. United States—Economic policy. I. Title.
SB950.3.L29M87   1994
363.17′92′098—dc20   94-14278

Library
University of Texas
at San Antonio

This book is dedicated to the memory of
Benjamin Linder and Mirna Mack Chang,
who gave their lives in the quest for a more just and humane world.

Contents

Figures

Tables

Preface

I first became interested in pesticides while conducting a study of social conflict in California agriculture (Murray 1982). Pesticide hazards and their resolution were the most common concern expressed by farm workers during field interviews designed to identify current and future issues around which farm workers were most likely to mobilize and organize.

In an effort to investigate these farm labor concerns further, I worked from 1980 to 1983 for the California Occupational Safety and Health (Cal/OSHA) program coordinating investigations of work-related illnesses and injuries caused by pesticides. During that period I first began to explore the broader dimensions of the technology's impact and the obstacles to addressing it. But it was not until 1983, when I initiated a nearly six-year effort to resolve pesticide-related health problems in Nicaragua, that I began to realize just how far-reaching the pesticide problems have been in the developing world. The rate of pesticide poisonings, the scope of pesticide contamination, and the economic and ecological disasters generated by heavy pesticide use were absolutely staggering in comparison to my U.S. experiences.

Over the ensuing ten years I worked closely with nongovernmental organizations, developing-country governments, and international development agencies on a variety of projects and studies to address pesticide problems in Latin America. Throughout this period, I grew increasingly aware of a much more extensive relationship between pesticides and the process of social change than has been commonly recognized among those trying to resolve the health, environmental, or production problems associated with pesticides. I gradually came to the conclusion that pesticide problems were an integral and constituent part of much broader problems facing the majority of people in the developing countries where I lived and worked.

Further, it became clear to me that the frequent failure (with important exceptions) of environmental, labor, and public health activists to locate pesticide problems within this broader context was an important reason the demands for pesticide reforms had a relatively marginal influence, not only on the course of chemical-intensive agriculture in the Third World but also on the postwar development process more generally. For example, if those environmental groups that recently embraced the North American Free Trade Agreement (Schneider 1993) understood the broad socioeconomic and ecological effects in rural Mexico of the pesticide-intensive agricultural development that will inevitably follow this accord, they might be less eager to applaud the free trade agreement. The experiences of Central American and Caribbean countries described in Chapters 4 and 5 are a clear warning of the problems in store for the Mexican peasantry in the free trade era. Similarly, the unfolding turmoil in Chiapas, Mexico, suggests what is at stake if fundamental changes are not made in development strategies more generally.

The location and analysis of pesticide problems in this greater context of development and social change is the immediate task of this book. The more fundamental goal is to link the pesticide problem and the efforts to resolve it with the broader changes that must occur if the future course of Latin American development is to be ecologically viable, economically sound, and socially just. Pesticide-based agricultural development has thus far failed to qualify on each and every count. If the pesticide problems are to be resolved, the course of Latin American development will by necessity have to change. If this book can make a small contribution to the broader process of change, it will have achieved its purpose.

A combination of research grants and consulting projects, including a Fulbright Central America Research Grant and a Ford Foundation collaborative research grant, allowed me to conduct many of the studies that are included in this book. But it was the John D. and Catherine T. MacArthur Foundation Program on Peace and International Cooperation, which provided a Research and Writing Grant for Individuals, that allowed me to devote the year of concentrated effort necessary to complete the research and write the first draft of this book. Without that support, this book would likely not have been written.

I am indebted to the staff and students at the Center for Latin American Studies at Stanford University for providing a stimulating and supportive institutional setting in which to write. The center's director, Terry Karl, has created one of the most exciting and productive intellectual environments I have ever encountered in a university setting. Dr. Karl also played an important role as an advisor and critic in the early stages of developing this book, and I am truly grateful for her professional guidance and personal friendship.

The list of individuals with whom I worked on various studies that have contributed to this book is endless, and I apologize for not being able to include them all. During my years in Nicaragua, I worked closely with Donald Cole, Dale Harrison, Ricardo Ibañez, Rob McConnell, Nellie Torres, Merri Weinger, and the personnel of the Nicaraguan Ministry of Health, Department of León. More recently, Michael Conroy and Peter Rosset have been key collaborators in much of the research on nontraditional agriculture that has gone into this book, and they share credit, where any is due, for the success of this project. Similarly, the research teams that conducted the Ford Foundation–funded study of nontraditional agriculture in Central America, including the researchers at the Asociación para el Avance de las Ciencias Sociales in Guatemala, Programa Regional de Investigación sobre El Salvador, the Posgrado de Economía y Planificacíon at the National Autonomous University of Honduras, the Centro de Investigaciones Economicas y Sociales and the Department of Agricultural Economics of the National Autonomous University of Nicaragua, and the Centro de Capacitación para el Desarrollo in Costa Rica, were critical to the generation of the primary data in Chapters 4 and 5.

The reviewers for the University of Texas Press, John H. Perkins and Angus Wright, were very helpful with the revision of this manuscript, as were the guidance and editorial assistance of Jan McInroy and Lorraine Atherton of the University of Texas Press. Many helpful comments and suggestions were also provided by Peter Davis, Laura Enriquez, Monica Moore, Rob McConnell, and Sean Swezey. The Pesticide Action Network of North America's Information Clearinghouse has been a frequent and valuable resource during the development of this book.

A note on intellectual debt is also appropriate at this point. Much of the historical background in this book has been drawn from a growing body of excellent research into socioeconomic development, particularly in Central America. This includes the works of Victor Bulmer-Thomas, Charles Brockett, and most notably Robert Williams. Similarly, the analysis in this book has been influenced by several classic studies in pesticide problems by Rachel Carson, David Weir and Mark Shapiro, and David Bull, as well as by more recent works by Angus Wright, Sean Swezey, Keith Andrews, and Jeffery Bentley, among others. I have tried to expand upon this body of research by providing a detailed analysis of a specific set of pesticide problems in a geographical and historical context. I have blended a considerable amount of data and personal experience, much of it presented for the first time, and built upon the analyses provided by earlier scholarship. To the degree that I have provided some greater understanding of the problems treated in this book, I am indebted to the work of those named and unnamed who have pursued these questions before me.

Finally, I am grateful to my compañera, Dana Walker, for her patience and support, and to our son, Daniel Walker-Murray, for constantly reminding me of the important things in life.

1

Development's Unkept Promise

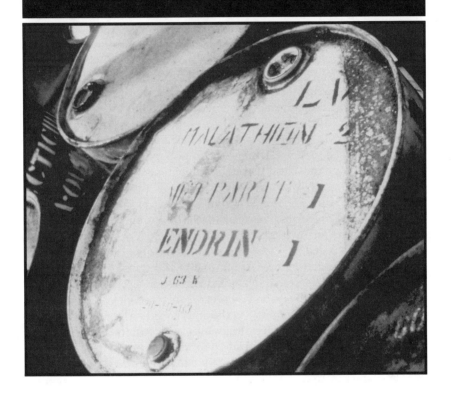

The United States emerged from the Second World War with a mission. U.S. policymakers developed an ambitious agenda for the modernization of those regions of the world that lacked the social, economic, and political structures and processes deemed essential to the success of Western developed societies (of which the United States was considered an ideal-typical example). The need for fundamental changes seemed undeniable. Poverty and disease were endemic in many regions of the world, and their rates were rising. Economic growth was marginal at best, and viable social welfare systems were rarities (at least by Western standards). Ever-expanding population pressures combined with limited food production capacities warned of increasing hunger, despair, and discontent, which could fuel social and political instability.

For U.S. policymakers, the specter of spreading communism in the postwar era added to, if not defined, the importance of an expanding U.S. role in developing the Third World. Development was seen as critical to alleviating the array of social problems and in turn denying external subversive elements a fertile terrain in which to promote instability in the Third World countries. Premised in part on the successes of the Marshall Plan in the reconstruction of war-torn Europe, the promise of development was based on a profound faith in the organizational prowess of capitalist state and market forces, and in the transformative powers of modern science and technology. Industrial and agricultural modernization were seen as the necessary precursors to stable, pluralistic, and democratic societies. According to the emerging development discourse of the postwar era,[1] once the less developed societies achieved the proper mix of economic and social changes they would "take off," developing into dynamic, and increasingly equal, members of the modern world order (Huntington 1968; Lipset and Solari 1967; Rostow 1960).

Agriculture was particularly important to the new development scheme, insofar as it was the means to increase food production and raise nutritional levels, thus providing relief from disease and hunger. Agricultural development also offered, according to development planners, a relatively quick means of generating the capital necessary to drive Third World industrialization (Kaimowitz 1992). In addition, increasing development could create rising demand for U.S. exports at a time when U.S. productive capacity was at a historic high, nearly double its prewar levels, as well as provide an expanding volume and variety of raw materials and commodities to meet the needs of America's industrial heartland and growing middle class. Further, when U.S. productivity generated commodity surpluses or outmoded technologies, these developing economies provided profitable outlets to alleviate production bottlenecks and profit realization crises.

An array of development policies and technological measures were implemented to increase productivity and modernize the agrarian sectors of the Third World. The central component of these efforts was the promotion of the Green Revolution, a strategy premised on agricultural modernization in part through the breeding of "high response" plant varieties. These new varieties generated greater crop yields when combined with technological advances such as elaborate irrigation systems, tractors and farm machinery, and agrochemicals (pesticides and fertilizers) (Cleaver 1974; Jennings 1988; Pearse 1980). The Green Revolution and the technology-intensive farming it fostered promised to defuse the Malthusian time bomb of Third World populations growing faster than their capacity to feed themselves. Increasing food production was considered essential to reducing the social tensions and population-related problems.

This development strategy relied on pesticides as the primary or virtually exclusive form of pest control.[2] With relatively inexpensive chemical inputs, it was argued, crop yields would rise and new crops could be introduced where various pests had previously made agricultural diversification impossible. Pesticides were heralded as a miracle technology[3] without which, in the long run, farmers could not expect to be efficient and viable participants in the modernization process. Norman Borlaug, "the father of the Green Revolution," deemed pesticides to be such an unassailable cornerstone of modern development that he argued, "We can either use the fertilizers and pesticides available to us, or we can starve" (Boardman 1986).

U.S. development efforts grew steadily after the Second World War, bringing the miracles of modern agriculture to ever more remote areas of the world. By the 1980s, billions of dollars in U.S. development assistance had helped spread advanced technological packages throughout the Third World, including the annual donation or financing of pesticides worth tens of millions of dollars. Development was literally being poured onto the Third World.

When groups and individuals began to question the wisdom of the increasing dependence on pesticides, they were met by a powerful and incessant chorus of scientists, politicians, and others who sang the praises of the miracle technology. A passage from the 1981 annual report of Bayer Chemical Company captures the tone of several decades of responses to those opposing unbridled promotion of chemical-intensive agriculture: "In view of the challenge posed by world hunger, emotional attacks against conscientious agricultural chemicals research are attacks against humanity" (Barry 1987:91).

But today, little more than four decades after the "rush to develop" (Bulmer-Thomas 1987) began, the promise of development has not been realized. As one observer concluded, "The dream is over; development, as it was promised in the midst of post-War euphoria, has not happened. Moreover, the 'Third World' is more Third World than ever, more 'underdeveloped' now than when it was discovered to be so" (Escobar 1988:1). Poverty has increased in many regions of the world, along with social and political instability. Social inequity, the gap between rich and poor, has widened as the benefits of economic development have reached a far smaller portion of the world's population than initial forecasts had predicted (UNDP 1991).

Nor have the expectations of modern science and the advanced technologies been met. Countries that historically produced most or all of their basic dietary needs before pursuing modern agricultural development now import increasing amounts of food, causing escalating debt obligations, which these countries cannot meet. Per capita food production actually declined in Africa and Latin America during this development era (Holl et al. 1990:341). Nutritional levels fell for many as well, even as Third World economies grew. The daily caloric consumption of several million Guatemalan Indians, for example, is today lower than it was at the time of the Conquest five hundred years ago, in spite of (or, as this book will argue, at least in part because of) four decades of U.S. agricultural development assistance.

Today pests destroy an estimated 37 percent of all potential food and fiber crops, a rate that approximates the losses that occurred before the widespread use of pesticides (Pimentel and Lehman 1993). Meanwhile, chemical contamination of food, water, and soil is becoming an increasing problem throughout many agricultural zones, and pesticide-related health problems now rival some of the most serious diseases in the Third World (Jeyaratnam 1990; McConnell 1988; Wright 1990).

It appears that the ambitious development agenda of the postwar era has not only failed to achieve the modernization of the Third World but has instead generated a profound and far-reaching crisis. The role of pesticides as a central technology in these development efforts demonstrates how the means to achieve the vision of modernization have paradoxically led to the very antithesis of that dream, a deeper and more intractable immiseration of Third World societies.

Nowhere has the role of pesticides been more significant in Third World development than in Latin America. Throughout much of the past four decades, Latin America has been a leading market for the entire range of agrochemicals. Central America alone accounted for 40 percent of U.S. pesticide exports to the Western Hemisphere during the cotton boom in the 1960s (Vaughn and Leon 1977). With the takeoff of the new development process based on nontraditional agricultural exports, many Caribbean and Central American crops have grown even more dependent on pesticides. Thus these regions represent an ideal focus for analyzing the technology's relationship to, and role in, the agrarian changes occurring throughout the developing world. The lessons drawn from the Latin American case studies in this book are not significantly different from those one would expect to learn from studies of other parts of the developing world, and in some ways they may represent a vision of things to come in those other regions.

Why have the pervasive problems caused by pesticides persisted in Latin America? The answer for the regions analyzed in this book lies in large part in the coevolution of the chemical technology and one particular crop. As we will see in Chapters 2 and 3, many of the problems found in Latin America today are at least partially rooted in the postwar boom of both pesticide and cotton production.

Yet the study of pesticides and cotton is really only a study of origins, and a partial one at that. Why has the pesticide problem persisted, and even grown, while cotton has all but disappeared from many parts of Latin America? The answer to this question in part lies in the promotion of new chemically dependent crops, most notably the "nontraditional agricultural exports" analyzed in Chapters 4 and 5. The new crops are not only re-creating many of the pesticide problems seen in cotton but are also generating pesticide-related crises at a rate faster than occurred during the cotton era.

But the persistence of the problem can also be attributed to the very efforts to resolve it, both through alternative pest-control strategies (Chapter 6) and through the pursuit of "safe use" strategies (Chapter 7). As I will argue by way of conclusion (Chapter 8), the efforts to resolve the pesticide problem in Latin America and elsewhere have largely remained trapped in a traditional development paradigm maximizing short-term growth with little regard for or understanding of longer-term sustainability and broader social and ecological dynamics.

Finally, I will argue that several efforts under way in Latin America suggest more fundamental solutions to pesticide and development problems. The ultimate resolution of the pesticide problem will require strengthening these countertendencies while bringing an end to the promotion of an unsustainable course of development.

2

Pesticides and the Central American Cotton Boom

My first visit to the cotton fields of Latin America was a memorable one. In early 1983 I drove from Nicaragua's capital city of Managua to León, the departmental center of the largest cotton-growing area in Central America. As I drove north along the highway, I passed mile after mile of cotton plants draped in maturing cotton bolls, which hung from the tall green stalks like white Spanish moss. Nearing León, I passed dozens of trucks and tractors pulling long trailers filled with barrels of pesticides destined for the dirt airstrips on the nearby farms, to be loaded into the spray planes. World War I–vintage biplanes swooped down across the road ahead, spraying yellow and green clouds of chemicals onto cotton fields growing right up to the roadside.

Near the city of León, I saw a long line of billboards touting the wonders of an array of pesticide products. As I passed through the city, I saw stores, seemingly on every corner, advertising the sale of pesticide products. In the patios or doorways of many houses stood empty 55-gallon pesticide barrels, which the residents used to store food, water, or other materials. In some places, barrels had been pounded flat to use for roofing material or for outside walls of homes.

But the most lasting impression of my first venture into Central America's cotton sector was not the pervasive visual presence of the chemical technology nor even the vast sea of "white gold" that spread through the region. It was the smell of pesticides that hung so heavy on the air. The stench of these chemicals permeated the region and stayed with me for hours as I drove from La Paz Centro on the southern edge of the cotton farms, through the city of León, and north past the town of Chinandega. Indeed, the smell had become such a part of rural life and culture in the cotton region that Father Ernesto Cardenal, the famous Nicaraguan poet, recorded its effect in his poem "Lights." Cardenal, describing his clandestine return to Nicaragua from exile just before the overthrow of the Somoza dictatorship in 1979, wrote:

Now we're close to León, the territory liberated.
A burning reddish-orange light, like the red-hot tip of a cigar:
    Corinto:
the powerful lights of the docks flickering on the sea.
And now at last the beach at Poneloya, and the plane coming in
    to land,

the string of foam along the coast gleaming in the moonlight.
The plane coming down. A smell of insecticide.
And Sergio tells me: "The smell of Nicaragua!"

So this analysis of the role of pesticides in Latin American development must first examine the intimate linkages between cotton and pesticides and try to reveal how together they became such an integral part of Central American reality.

Pesticides play an important role in the cultivation of a wide range of crops in Latin America. From coffee to corn, bananas to beans, the technology is without question a key element in agricultural production. Export crops, with their often year-round, technology-intensive, mono-cultural production systems, are particularly dependent upon pesticides. For example, bananas, a key export for several Central and South American economies, are treated with a significant portion of the total volume of pesticides applied in these countries. Seventy-five percent of the pesticides used in Honduras (Molina 1989) and 35 percent of the pesticides used in Costa Rica are sprayed on bananas (Trivelato and Wesseling 1991 : 2). Other countries with a dependence on one or more export crops have developed a similar pattern of concentrated use of the technology in the agroexport sector.

Yet one crop has historically accounted for far more pesticide use than any other, not only in Latin America but also throughout much of the developing world. Cotton, for several decades after World War II, consumed roughly 25 percent of the entire volume of global pesticide use (Bull 1982).[1] No other crop has played such an important role in the development of pesticides in the Third World or in the rise of the problems now associated with their continued use.

The Rise of Cotton in Latin America

Cotton is indigenous to Latin America, reportedly originating in Central America and the West Indies (ICAITI 1977 : 178). The oldest documented evidence of cotton production, however, comes from the Indus River Valley in what is now Pakistan, where cotton cloth was found from the period 3000 B.C. (Lewis and Richmond 1968). The earliest evidence of cotton cultivation in Latin America comes from remnants of cotton fabric found in Peru, dating back to 2500 B.C. By the time of the Conquest during the early to mid sixteenth century, cotton was being grown and cotton clothing was being traded in various parts of South America. Spanish soldiers encountered Aztec warriors using woven cotton armor, which the Spaniards found to be superior to their own in the region's tropical climate (Stein 1957). West Indian cotton subsequently became an important element in the rise of England as a world power. In 1787 over half of English cotton came from the West Indies (Wolf 1982:278–279). By 1807 England's primary source of cotton had shifted to the United States, which provided 60 percent of British cotton imports. Cotton production became the driving force in U.S. expansion after 1815 and represented over half the value of U.S. exports until 1860. United States cotton production rose dramatically during this period, from only 3,000 bales (a bale equals 500 pounds of lint cotton) in 1790 to 4.5 million bales in 1860 (Fogel and Engerman 1974:44).

By the nineteenth century, cotton was important to Latin America as well, with Brazil, Peru, and Mexico becoming significant exporters to England, the United States, and elsewhere. Latin American cotton production continued to expand during the American Civil War, particularly in Peru (Wolf 1982:377). After 1892 Mexican cotton production also became profitable in the international economy with the introduction of a U.S. seed variety. Mexican production increased rapidly in the early twentieth century, from 58,000 bales in 1901–1902 to 170,000 bales in 1906–1907 (Clark 1909:28).

Central America was the source of a limited amount of cotton during the colonial era, with Nicaragua producing sailcloth for the great ships of the European powers (Enriquez 1991:34). Central America also exported cotton to New York during the Civil War, although production stopped soon after the end of the conflict (Williams 1986:14–15). The governments of Guatemala and El Salvador promoted cotton production in the region during the latter half of the nineteenth century, even though the only cotton mill, in Quezaltenango, Guatemala, continued to rely heavily on cotton imports from Peru, Mexico, and the United States (Clark 1909). By the early twentieth century most countries in Central and South America produced cotton on a limited scale or had local textile industries processing cotton from neighboring countries.

Early Obstacles to Cotton Production

Cotton production, like most crops, depended on several natural conditions. Relatively rich soil and hot, sunny climates were abundant throughout many parts of Latin America. But water was an important limiting factor as cotton required a considerable amount of moisture in the soil during the early stages of the growing cycle. Therefore cotton production was constrained in many areas by the ability to maintain adequate irrigation systems. In some regions, such as the Central American Pacific Coastal Plain stretching from Tapachula in southern Mexico to the Guanacaste of Costa Rica (Figure 2-1), the rainy season

Figure 2-1   Principal Cotton Areas in Central America.

was accompanied by monsoonlike downpours, which meant that no irrigation was necessary since the soil held ample moisture during much
of the growing season to allow cotton plants to thrive. It also meant
there was considerable yearly variation in productivity. In years when
rainfall was light and again in years when heavy rain lasted weeks or
months later than normal, cotton quality and yields were lower because
of excessive moisture or other rain-related damage to the crop.

Unfortunately the hot, low-lying plains so conducive to cotton cultivation were also plagued by disease. Mayan populations had flourished
in the tropical lowlands until the Spanish merchants and Italian soldiers
who arrived during the Conquest and early colonial period brought malaria to the New World (Wolf 1982:133). The surviving Indian communities were forced to higher elevations (Avery 1985). Subsequent efforts
at large-scale, labor-dependent agriculture on the coastal plains were
inhibited by the risks of illness and death to both workers and landowners from tropical diseases. Nineteenth-century ventures into cotton

production on the Salvadoran coastal plain, for example, were quickly brought to a halt by malaria and yellow fever (Brockett 1988 : 45).

Yet the problems of disease and unpredictable weather paled in comparison to the main impediment to Central American cotton production, the boll weevil, *Anthonomus grandis* Boheman. No other single factor could approach the boll weevil in terms of destructive effects and ability to limit cotton production to a modestly profitable endeavor at best. The boll weevil, like cotton, appears to be indigenous to Latin America (Warner and Smith 1968). While exploring a cave near Mitla, Mexico, archeologists found several fragments of cultivated cotton. They were part of the materials left behind by native people who inhabited the site at about A.D. 900. Among the fragments were cotton bolls and several cotton seeds. The excavating scientists found one seed with a curiously familiar perforation. When the seed was broken open, it revealed a well-preserved boll weevil, effectively demonstrating that the insect had evolved in the region along with the plant and had dined on the human efforts at cotton cultivation for at least a thousand years.

The boll weevil, and to a lesser degree several other pests,[2] repeatedly constrained the development of large-scale cotton production in many Latin American countries. Robert Williams noted the role of the boll weevil, locally known as the *picudo*, in nineteenth-century Guatemala: "In the 1870s some enterprising Guatemalan landowners attempted to raise cotton on a large scale to supply Guatemala's first modern cotton mill. According to the reports, 'The efforts of these progressive farmers . . . were dashed by a plague of insects commonly called the picudo, against which they had no means of combat'" (Williams 1986 : 17).

In 1908, a special agent from the U.S. Department of Commerce and Labor toured Latin America to assess its potential for cotton development. In Mexico he observed that pests remained a significant obstacle to cotton production, noting, "The planters take great interest in the efforts that are being made by the Department of Agriculture in the United States to discover some enemy of the boll weevil, for if successful there would be rendered available for cotton cultivation large tracts of coast land on the Gulf and on the Pacific" (Clark 1909 : 29). Similarly, after visiting Nicaragua he concluded, "It would seem that all told there is not much over 50,000 acres in Nicaragua available for this purpose [cotton production], and already both the 'langosta'[3] and the 'picudo' are beginning to wax numerous and will do much to prevent any large extension" (Clark 1909 : 62).

Various techniques were employed for controlling the boll weevil in Latin America. Among the most common were handpicking the pest from the cotton plants or just relying on natural enemies of the insect to keep the pest and pest damage to an acceptable level. So-called progressive producers began emulating cotton growers of the American South in the late nineteenth and early twentieth centuries, applying chemicals such as sulfur and nicotine, in the form of an infusion of tobacco leaves, which provided limited control of the pest (ICAITI 1977:28).

In the United States, cotton farmers continued to search for chemical controls of the boll weevil, which had migrated into the American South from Mexico in the latter half of the nineteenth century (Dunlap 1981). In the early 1900s the Bureau of Entomology of the United States Department of Agriculture (USDA) found that a fine dust of calcium arsenate provided good control and began touting the pesticide. Almost overnight calcium arsenate became the primary means of weevil control. Sales of the chemical jumped from 50,000 pounds produced by one company in 1918 to 10 million pounds a year produced by twenty companies only two years later (Dunlap 1981:30). By 1935 the United States was producing 43,295,354 pounds of the compound (Dunlap 1981:253).

Latin American producers quickly followed their American counterparts, and calcium arsenate became a mainstay of cotton pest control from Mexico to Brazil. But those early insecticide applications had only limited effect in the more tropical regions, in part because heavy rains, which occur during the period when the pests begin to cause significant damage, quickly washed the poisons off the plants. Since these compounds depended upon the boll weevil's ingesting the insecticide, their efficacy was greatly hindered by the weather.

The boll weevil and other factors combined to keep prewar cotton yields to an average of 1,550 kilograms per hectare (kg/ha) in Central America (ICAITI 1977:28). Yields from this region remained somewhat behind those of the American South, and cotton production for the international market was often profitable only during periods of international shortage or peak market prices (Enriquez 1991).

The Technological Breakthrough

In 1939 a Swiss research team made a major scientific breakthrough in the development of the chemical pest control technology. Paul Müller, working for the J. R. Geigy Company, found the insecticidal properties of a previously developed compound, 1,1,1 trichloro-2, 2bis(parachlorophenyl) ethane, or DDT, to be far superior to any pesticides previously tested (Dunlap 1981).

Besides being far more potent than existing products, the new compound could kill pests through contact and absorption, in addition to ingestion. It also had lasting effects, killing insects months after its application. It was insoluble in water, did not break down quickly in sunlight, and oxidized slowly, thus making it particularly appealing for tropical climates (Williams 1986:17). DDT soon received the close attention of the USDA and the U.S. military. In 1942, the War Food Administration tested Müller's compound and quickly put it to use. Contrary to the name of the agency, it first employed DDT not for food but for military purposes. Malaria was the single biggest health problem in the South Pacific, accounting for five times the casualties caused by enemy action (Blodgett 1974:207). Soldiers and civilians in other war zones such as northern Africa and parts of Europe were facing similar hazards from a variety of insect-borne diseases.

In 1943 an epidemic of typhus broke out in Naples. American and British occupation authorities began dusting exposed persons to control body lice, the disease vector (Dunlap 1981:62). By February 1944, three million individual dustings of DDT or pyrethrum (a botanical insecticide) had been administered to civilians and soldiers, and for the first time in history a typhus epidemic was halted by public health measures. Spectacular results were also being achieved in the South Pacific where the military employed bombers and transport planes to blanket the islands with DDT spray, drastically reducing the incidence of malaria.

Public awareness of the new compound spread rapidly, with newspapers and the popular media heralding DDT as a miracle insecticide. *Popular Science's* account was typical: "At last science has found the weapons for total victory on the insect front. . . . It will unlock the doors to vast areas where disease-bearing insects have barred the way to development and progress" (Sinks 1944:56A-B). The U.S. surgeon general speculated that the compound might mean the end of insect-borne diseases (Dunlap 1981:62). Similarly, USDA's Sievert A. Rohwer reported in December 1944, "We feel that never in the history of entomology [has] a chemical been discovered that offers such promise to mankind for relief from his insect problems as DDT" (Perkins 1982:10), and *Science News Letter* (1945) predicted DDT would "send malaria mosquitoes, typhus lice and other disease-carrying insects to join the dodo and the dinosaur in the limbo of extinct species, thereby ending these particular plagues for all time."

By the end of 1944 American manufacturers were producing more than two million pounds of DDT per month under contract with the U.S. government, reaching a production level of three million pounds a month by war's end the following year (Dunlap 1981:60). As did many other industries, U.S. chemical companies like Monsanto, Hercules, DuPont, and Merck found themselves with a large production capacity built upon wartime demand for the technology. On August 1, 1945, the War Production Board released DDT for general civilian use, once production levels had exceeded military requirements.

The industry's impressive profits from wartime sales of DDT spurred the search for other synthetic organic compounds. From 1945 to 1953 an estimated twenty-five new pesticides were introduced, including BHC (benzene hexachloride), chlordane, toxaphene, aldrin, dieldrin, endrin, heptachlor, parathion, methyl parathion, and tetraethyl pyrophosphate (Perkins 1982 : 10). Building on the high level of public recognition of DDT, the chemical industry introduced the new products to U.S. and Third World farmers with great fanfare. As one food company official later commented, "The publicity given DDT might well be envied by any Hollywood movie star" (Brittin 1950 : 594).

Much of the publicity was well deserved, as impressive yields were obtained throughout a wide range of crops:

> The reports of spectacular successes came from all agricultural areas. Apple growers in the Yakima Valley of Washington saw their losses from codling moth drop from 15 percent with lead arsenate to 3–5 percent with DDT. Potato growers found that DDT helped increase their yields from 155 bushels per acre (1945) to 211 bushels per acre (1949). Cotton growers in Louisiana, heavily plagued with the boll weevil since the first decade of the century, found that toxaphene and other new insecticides controlled the weevil far better than calcium arsenate, the only material with even moderate effectiveness up to that time. (Perkins 1980 : 26–27)

Pesticide sales jumped from $40 million in 1939 to $260 million in 1954 (Dunlap 1981 : 73), as chemical manufacturing became "the premier industry of the U.S." (Perkins 1982 : 13). The number of pesticide companies grew from 83 to 275 during that same period, and DuPont, Union Carbide, Dow, Allied, and Monsanto became the giants of the U.S. chemical industry. Meanwhile, in 1948 Paul Müller received the Nobel prize in physiology and medicine.

Latin American cotton farmers were quick to adopt the innovations occurring in the U.S. cotton industry. By the end of the 1940s the new synthetic organic compounds were becoming an integral part of cotton farming throughout the hemisphere. For example, following a poor cotton harvest in 1949, producers in the Cañete Valley of Peru turned to DDT, BHC, and toxaphene to control bollworms, aphids, leafworms, and bud weevils (Barducci 1972 : 429–430). Cotton production increased dramatically, and by 1954 yields were double the 1949 level.

Central Americans found the new chemicals equally effective. During the 1940s the entire region produced about 25,000 bales of cotton annually, almost entirely for regional consumption (Williams 1986 : 14). Near the end of the decade cotton growers began introducing the new chemicals. Salvadoran farmers found that the aerial spraying of pesticides was both effective and economical, and they were soon followed by other Central American producers in the introduction of high-technology pest control measures. By the 1950s DDT was widely used throughout Guatemala, El Salvador, and Nicaragua for the control of several cotton pests. DDT, in this case, was not very effective for boll weevil control. Instead, toxaphene and, by the mid-fifties, parathion became the chemicals of choice for weevil control.

DDT also gave increasingly effective relief from malaria and other vector-borne diseases in the expanding lowland cotton fields of Central America's Pacific Coastal Plain. The World Health Organization (WHO) and national governments implemented pesticide spraying campaigns throughout these areas, which steadily reduced malaria rates over the first two decades after the end of the war. The reduction in disease further fueled the growth of Central America's cotton economy, as well as the growth of other parts of the agricultural export sector.

Pesticides were of course not the only factor influencing the expansion of cotton after World War II. Reconstruction in Europe and an expanding U.S. economy generated increasing worldwide demand for cotton. During the Korean War, considerable speculation on the fear of cotton shortages drove international market prices to record highs, further stimulating the global cotton economy. Latin American producers responded to the increased demands by rapidly expanding production during the early 1950s. The rising agricultural commodity prices spurred vigorous capitalization of Central American agriculture as more and more farmers turned to pesticides and other high technology farming strategies. Some farmers became millionaires after a single cotton harvest (Williams 1986:16). The high market prices and reports of quick fortunes lured many entrepreneurs into the cotton industry. Yet without the ability to control cotton pests, as well as the ability to control the spread of malaria in the coastal lowlands being opened up to new cultivation, Central American cotton expansion would simply not have been sustainable (FAO 1990a:7).

Central American cotton production rose dramatically, albeit erratically, for three decades. During the 1950s cotton yields jumped from 1,550 kg/ha to 2,270 kg/ha (ICAITI 1977:29). Between 1948 and 1958, the area of cotton harvested increased more than eightfold, from 19,000 hectares to 164,000 hectares (Figure 2-2). Nicaragua, which had no more than 3,000 hectares under cultivation before 1949, expanded cotton farming to 74,000 hectares a decade later (Table 2-1) as cotton became a driving force behind national economic growth (Paige 1985:91).

In the 1960s Central American cotton production expanded at an impressive annual rate of 7.8 percent, to a regional average of 281,000 hectares (FAO 1990a:7). By the mid-1960s Nicaragua was the regional leader

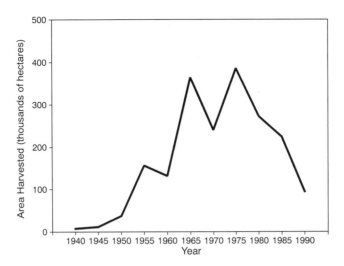

Figure 2-2 Central American Cotton Production, 1940–1990. *Source: FAO Production Yearbook.*

in cotton production with more than 150,000 hectares under cultivation. El Salvador and Guatemala followed with a combined total of 202,000 hectares in 1965. Nicaragua, Guatemala, and El Salvador produced 95 percent of the region's cotton by the end of the 1960s, and all three were among the world's twenty-four top cotton-producing nations (Table 2-2). Cotton became the cornerstone of regional development as Central America entered a "Golden Age" of economic growth (Bulmer-Thomas 1987). From 1965 to 1975 the regional gross domestic product grew at an annual rate of 4.9 percent (Brockett 1988:85). Regional revenues from cotton lint and cottonseed, domestic and export, reached $160 million in the mid-1960s and soared to nearly half a billion dollars by 1978 (Williams 1986:28). Central American cotton production peaked at 446,300 hectares in 1978, and the region's cotton yields were 153 percent of U.S. yields (FAO 1990a:1). The following year, cotton accounted for 14.5 percent of the region's entire foreign trade (Chapin and Wasserstrom 1983:119).

That narrow strip of coastal plain, which Special Agent Clark had described at the beginning of the century as overrun with boll weevils and malaria, was by 1978 the third leading source of cotton in the world, after the United States and Egypt (Williams 1986:14). Pesticides had made the cotton boom possible, not only in Central America but also around the world, and in the process cotton production became the most chemical-intensive and chemical-dependent agricultural activity in the international economy. As the Food and Agriculture Organization

Table 2-1 Central American Cotton Production, 1940–1990
Area Harvested (thousands of hectares)[a]

Year	Costa Rica	Nicaragua	El Salvador	Guatemala	Honduras	Total
1940	—	3	3	2	—	2
1941	—	6	3	3	—	12
1942	—	2	4	3	—	9
1943	—	2	5	—	—	7
1944	—	2	5	1	—	8
1945	—	2	10[b]	—	—	12
1946	—	—	11[b]	3	—	14
1947	—	—	15	3	—	18
1948	—	3	13	3	—	19
1949	—	15	17	3	—	35
1950	—	17	19	2	—	38
1951	—	35	30	8	—	73
1952	—	30	28	9	2	69
1953	—	42	21	11	2	76
1954	—	86	30	16	3	135
1955	—	87	46	21	2	156
1956	—	78	38	13	4	133
1957	—	61	40	18	7	126
1958	—	74	54	28	8	164
1959	—	67	39	18	2	126
1960	—	61	43	26	2	132
1961	—	78	77	46	2	203
1962	—	95	94	72	5	266
1963	—	119	119	91	7	336
1964	5	135	122	100	9	371
1965	7	142	98	104	14	365
1966	8	152	71	83	15	329
1967	7	147	53	85	14	306
1968	8	132	59	95	11	305
1969	4	109	53	83	12	261
1970	3	103	56	74	4	240
1971	3	95	62	71	4	235
1972	3	109	73	89	7	281
1973	3	136	85	89	8	321
1974	1	182	95	104	9	391
1975	0	179	88	111	8	386
1976	3	144	74	84	10	315
1977	14	198	79	122	10	423
1978	11	212	99	123	18	463
1979	8	174	102	122	11	417
1980	7	45	85	123	13	273
1981	8	94	58	100	8	268
1982	8	93	53	66	4	224
1983	3	116	49	56	6	230
1984	2	115	37	58	8	220
1985	2	115	37	63	7	224
1986	1	59	27	66	4	157
1987	2	60	13	31	4	110

Table 2-1 (*continued*)

Year	Costa Rica	Nicaragua	El Salvador	Guatemala	Honduras	Total
1988	2	41	13	40	4	100
1989	1	40	13	47	3	104
1990[c]	1	35	10	46	3	95
Total	125	4,127	2,428	2,635	284	9,599

[a] Unless otherwise noted, all data are from the annual *FAO Production Yearbook*.
[b] B. R. Mitchell, *International Historical Statistics: The Americas and Australasia* (Detroit: Gale Research Co., 1983).
[c] 1990 figures from the *1991 UN Statistical Yearbook for Latin America and the Caribbean*.

Table 2-2 Cotton Production in Major Producing Countries, 1967–1968 Season

Country	World rank	Thousands of bales	Thousands of hectares	Pounds per hectare
USSR	1	9,460	2,442	1,850
USA	2	7,215	3,236	1,104
China	3	7,000	5,059	661
India	4	5,330	8,215	311
Brazil	5	2,750	2,266	579
Pakistan	6	2,400	1,732	661
UAR	7	2,014	683	1,408
Mexico	8	2,000	689	1,388
Turkey	9	1,825	718	1,214
Sudan	10	900	486	883
Syria	11	585	240	1,167
Iran	12	545	291	894
Nicaragua	13	470	146	1,533
Colombia	14	465	174	1,273
Greece	15	443	138	1,540
Peru	16	390	155	1,416
Guatemala	17	360	89	1,924
Argentina	18	335	293	546
Tanzania	19	325	263	593
Spain	20	300	149	965
Uganda	21	285	868	159
Mozambique	22	195	316	297
Chad	23	175	297	282
El Salvador	24	160	45	1,683
Australia	25	150	29	2,485
Israel	26	131	30	2,137
Thailand	27	125	87	687
Nigeria	28	125	—	—
Afghanistan	29	90	121	352
World total		47,817	31,005	740

SOURCE: Smith and Reynolds 1972 : 375.

of the United Nations (FAO) observed in 1970, half the world's cotton production would have disappeared without the availability of pesticides (Bull 1982: 5).

Promoting Cotton in Central America

Governments and international development agencies played an important role in the growth of the cotton economy as well as in the proliferation of the agrochemical technology that sustained it. Once again, the experience of Central America provides the definitive example.

By the late 1940s Central American governments, from the progressive Arbenz regime to Somoza's autocracy, were financing new investment ventures in cotton cultivation through the infusion of state bank funds backed by U.S. and international lending institutions (Brockett 1988:46). In the 1950s private banks joined the state lenders, reaping a portion of the profits generated by the regional cotton boom through the 1960s and 1970s.

Cotton production was heavily dependent upon bank financing. Major capital outlays were necessary before planting and during the early stages of the cotton cycle. Seed, fertilizer, fuel for farm equipment, and pesticides locked up producer capital for six to eight months or more until the harvest was sold. Consequently, as many as 80 to 90 percent of Central American producers depended on bank loans to pursue cotton farming during the 1960s (Williams 1986:25). In Nicaragua, 94 percent of the cotton producers reportedly relied on private or state bank credits in the early 1980s (Colburn 1986:49).

Bank loans were often directly tied to crop yields (Paige 1985:100). In order to increase foreign exchange earnings, banks provided more-favorable credit rates and other incentives to producers achieving the highest yields, which stimulated the use of pesticides as farmers sought to reduce pest-related losses and maximize short-term returns on their investments. In addition, line items in loan contracts normally prescribed the types of chemicals and number of applications considered necessary for yield maximization, further stimulating pesticide use. In turn, agrochemicals became a greater part of farming expenses, driving producers to seek still more bank financing. Pesticide and fertilizer purchases and related application costs made up a third or more of producer costs (Enriquez 1991:36; Swezey et al. 1986:9; Williams 1986:18). Pesticide use was also encouraged through the development strategies of the international lending institutions and the local state and private banks. Various governments' direct and indirect subsidies of pesticide prices made pesticides ever more appealing.[4]

U.S. law prohibited direct financing of cotton production in Central

America when there were U.S. cotton surpluses (McCamant 1968:219). Nevertheless, much of the agricultural assistance to Guatemala, El Salvador, and Nicaragua found its way into the cotton economy, and a significant part of that assistance went into the purchase of pesticides for cotton. A portion of U.S. aid under the Alliance for Progress and other development assistance to Central American banks was intended to provide credits for basic grain production and other domestic and smaller-scale agricultural activities, but the Central American banks used this financing to make loans almost entirely directed at larger producers in cotton and cattle.

For example, in the mid-1960s, the U.S. Agency for International Development (USAID) made a $9 million loan to Nicaragua through the Basic Food Crop Program for the purchase of pesticides for basic grain producers (Dosal 1985:88). The loans financed the purchase of pesticides manufactured in the United States, but with no control over who could purchase the pesticides and virtually no available credits to basic grain producers to allow them to purchase these pesticides, there was little hope that the chemicals reached the intended recipients. In 1965, just before the loan, Nicaragua used a total of $10 million in pesticides, with 87 percent of that amount spent solely on insecticides for cotton (Swezey et al. 1986:8). It is unlikely that the $9 million the U.S. government provided to finance pesticide purchases the following year did anything more than subsidize cotton producer inputs and spur Nicaraguan cotton production, as well as generate additional sales for U.S. chemical companies.

U.S. government assistance became a central component of the efforts to promote the use of pesticides, not only in Central America but also throughout the developing world. From 1969 to 1974, USAID provided an annual average of $17.5 million in grants and loans for the purchase of pesticides (Bull 1982:74). In 1970 alone USAID financed $28.1 million of pesticide purchases, which represented 13.9 percent of all U.S. overseas pesticide sales (Milius and Morgan 1976). In some instances USAID financed 100 percent of the annual U.S. pesticide exports to a given country. With such extensive U.S. government support of pesticide purchases, the technology became an increasingly integral part of Central American agricultural development.

The Pesticide Industry in Central America

Not surprisingly, the Central American pesticide industry expanded during the cotton boom, driven both by direct financial assistance provided by the U.S. government and by private investment, with capital generated at least in part by cotton production. Most of the pesticide operations involved formulating plants, which imported technical-grade chemicals purchased from U.S. and European manufacturers and then formulated mixtures of these chemicals and packaged them under locally registered brand names.

The formulation of pesticides within Central America expanded during the first cotton boom of the 1950s. In 1952 pesticide distributors formulated 25 percent of their insecticide sales (Williams 1986:41). In 1955 they formulated 40 percent locally, and by 1959 the figure was 98 percent. This move to Central American–based operations was largely motivated by the international chemical industry's efforts to avoid local and regional import tariffs. With the rise of the Central American Common Market (CACM) in the 1960s and the adoption of regionwide exclusions from tariffs, chemical companies were able to sell their products in any of the five countries without paying additional tariffs.

Local investment groups, largely operating through local banks, invested in the Central American pesticide industry. The Banco Nicaragüense (Banic), with assets based primarily on the wealth of large cotton producers, invested in several pesticide distributors and manufacturers (Williams 1986:45–48). In El Salvador, cotton growers combined their fortunes with public-sector funds through the Banco Central de Reserva (Central Reserve Bank) and invested in pesticide companies and other pre- and post-harvest industries.

The expansion of pesticide formulation and manufacturing in Central America was also the result of U.S. financial assistance. In January 1963, the representatives of the CACM selected the first two projects to be provided regional tariff privileges under the Treaty on Central American Economic Integration of 1960 (McCamant 1968:253). Guatemala received approval for a tire and inner tube industry, and Nicaragua received approval for an insecticide plant and a caustic soda plant.

The Nicaraguan caustic soda plant (Elpesa) and the insecticide plant (Hercasa) were established by a consortium of investors brought together by USAID and the Instituto Nacional de Fomento (Infonac), an organization designed to promote investment. This latter organization was financed by the Inter-American Development Bank (IDB) (Dosal 1985). Infonac brought together investors from the Banic group, from a multinational investment group based in Luxembourg called the Adela Investment Company, and two U.S. chemical companies, Hercules Powder Company and Pennwalt Chemical Corporation. The venture was made appealing to investors through low-cost financing from USAID, the IDB, and the World Bank,[5] and by U.S. investment guarantees under the Investment Guarantee Program of USAID and later by the Overseas Private Investment Corporation (OPIC) (Dosal 1985:90).[6] Hercasa became the primary supplier of toxaphene for boll weevil control throughout Central America, on several occasions even supplying U.S. farmers with the pesticide.

By the late 1970s, pesticide-formulating facilities had developed in each of the Central American countries. Toxaphene manufacture by Hercasa in Nicaragua fell in the 1980s (Table 2-3) in response to mounting tension between the Sandinista government and the company and the declining effectiveness of the pesticide. Guatemala subsequently became the regional leader in pesticide manufacture and formulation, exporting over $45 million worth of pesticides in 1983.

What pesticides did for the expansion of cotton, cotton likewise did for pesticide sales in Central America. Cotton was the heaviest user of pesticides among all the major crops, both in the United States (Van den Bosch 1980) and in the Third World (WHO 1989). In Central America, it was estimated that as much as 85 percent of all the pesticides used in the region by the mid-1970s was applied to cotton (ICAITI 1977:212). With the initial rapid growth of cotton in the 1950s and 1960s, sales of U.S. pesticides soared in the region. By the peak of the first wave of cotton expansion in the mid-1960s, Central America was consuming 40 percent of all U.S. pesticide exports to the Western Hemisphere (Vaughn and Leon 1977).

Insecticides were the primary category of pesticide used in cotton, representing 80 percent or more of all pesticide use in some countries (ICAITI 1977; Swezey et al. 1986:8). In Nicaragua, insecticide sales jumped from $5.5 million in 1962–1963 to $11 million just two seasons later in 1964–1965 (Williams 1986:40). Pesticide use declined along

Table 2-3 Hercasa Production Data from Selected Years

Year	Production capacity (%)	Total sales (hundred thousand pounds)	Sales in Nicaragua (hundred thousand pounds)	Pounds toxaphene/hectare cotton (Nicaragua)
1974	100.8	20.84	—	—
1975	74.5	16.21	—	—
1980	46.1	8.97	—	—
1985	17.2	6.45	5.95	68.50
1986	12.0	4.49	4.19	64.32
1987	7.5	2.82	2.67	44.27
1988	3.2	1.21	1.21	28.86
1989	1.7	0.64	0.64	16.08

SOURCE: Appel et al. 1991.

with cotton hectarage in the latter part of the 1960s but increased again in the 1970s. As cotton expanded, and as oil price increases drove up pesticide prices in the mid-1970s, the value of insecticide sales rapidly rose again. In 1972–1973, the three main cotton-producing countries purchased $38 million in insecticides. Sales jumped to $60 million the next year and $107 million the next. By 1977–1978 sales reached $145 million. Pesticide use for the entire region reached 71,777,200 pounds of active ingredient in 1978, with insecticides still representing over 85 percent of the total volume (Leonard 1987: 226–227). Latin America became the heaviest user of pesticides per hectare in the Third World (Edwards 1986), with Central American cotton being a large contributor to this high level of chemical consumption.

The pesticide industry also became the driving force behind the increasing awareness of and positive attitudes about pesticide technology throughout the Central American agrarian sector. The promotion of modern, high-technology farming at the field level had historically been hindered by a lack of trained technicians in the region. Agricultural research and training, agricultural extension programs, and the general infrastructure of public-sector agricultural services were poorly developed, and repeated efforts at strengthening such systems were of limited success (McCamant 1968). The chemical companies, in contrast to the ineffective and oftentimes inept public-sector measures, became increasingly successful at educating producers and raising awareness more generally in the rural areas about the benefits to be gained from chemical technology. In so doing, the chemical industry effectively substituted advanced technology-linked knowledge for the knowledge and traditional practices employed in the rural areas before the pesticide promotional campaigns.

Companies established networks of trained salespeople and agricultural technicians throughout the region who worked with growers, government technicians, and officials, promoting the latest innovations in chemical pest control. As one agricultural researcher observed: "Those pesticide boys are all over the place down there. It's amazing how they get down to the grassroots" (Weir and Shapiro 1981: 41). In Guatemala, for example, chemical sales representatives were the primary and often exclusive source of pest control information as well as user training and education in the countryside (Campos 1986).

Sales personnel used a variety of incentives to sell their products, from handing out free baseball caps, with company logos or product line boldly displayed, to lavish parties and other monetary and nonmonetary inducements to producers and government officials. But incentives in the early days probably had less to do with the dramatic increase in pesticide use than the widely circulated stories of increased yields and overnight fortunes.

In addition, chemical salespeople helped promote the dominant pest control paradigm of the day, which called for total eradication of the pests. At the first sign of pest problems farmers were encouraged to call in the spray planes to douse their fields and eliminate any potential risk. Most pesticide users relied on regularly scheduled applications, or calendar spraying, which they found easier to maintain than scouting their fields for actual pest problems.

Chemical company promotional efforts spread from the fields to the training and education centers and into the government ministries and financial institutions as well. The technology had become the centerpiece of modern farming in Central America, and few questioned its importance in the booming cotton industry and in the region's consequent economic growth.

Conclusion

Pesticides created the ecological transformation necessary for the rapid expansion of cotton production after World War II. By controlling the boll weevil and other pests, Central American countries raised their cotton yields to levels equal to or higher than those of other major producing countries in the international market. Through the control of malaria and other vector-borne diseases on the Pacific Coastal Plain, they overcame other barriers to successful cotton production. As the cotton industry grew, so too did the chemical industry. The technology became a unifying thread between national and international investors seeking to tap into the new wealth being generated in the region as a wide range of political and economic interests found pesticides to be a central ingredient of their financial success.

Pesticides became such an important part of the boom in export agriculture that the technology appeared to be an unquestionable fixture in the modernization of these Third World economies and societies. As Father Cardenal's poetry demonstrated, pesticides became not only a part of the economic development process but a part of the culture and folklore of rural society as well.

It seemed for a time that the Golden Age of Central American development would continue indefinitely as cotton spread throughout the region, but the ecology of cotton production created by the new technology was not an ecology that could be maintained forever. By the end of the 1970s, it came into conflict with both human and environmental well-being in the region and began to undermine the foundations of the

Central American cotton boom. The agrochemical technology began to create the antithesis of the fast fortunes seen in the early days of the cotton boom in Central America as the region slipped into a complex pattern of interrelated ecological, economic, and social crisis. The crisis was not entirely nor even primarily created by pesticides, but once its pattern was set in motion, pesticides became a dynamic factor as the crisis drove Central America from a period of unprecedented economic expansion into a period of the greatest social and economic turmoil in the region's modern history.

3

Cotton and the Pesticide Crisis

Soon after my arrival in Nicaragua, I accompanied several health and safety inspectors from the Nicaraguan Ministry of Labor on an inspection of an airport at the edge of the city of Chinandega. The airfield was the largest of the more than one hundred airstrips in Nicaragua's cotton region. At these sites large quantities of concentrated pesticides were routinely mixed with water or other chemicals and loaded into airplanes to be sprayed on the cotton fields, an activity that daily exposed workers to considerable risk during the spraying season, from September to January.

As we approached the airport the now familiar stench of chemicals became overpowering. As we walked down the airstrip to the health clinic in the airport complex, I glanced across the adjacent fields toward the nearby dwellings of town. Nothing was moving in the open space, not birds, not insects, none of the creatures normally found in such abundance in these tropical climates. Here indeed, Rachel Carson's prophecy seemed all too real.

At the health clinic, which served the 125 workers at the airport, the nurse provided us with the injury and accident report for the previous month, October 1983. Having been a Cal/OSHA inspector for several years, I was accustomed to reviewing such reports, which normally included a log of various minor accidents along with the occasional fall, broken bone, or other more serious injury. The injury log was the normal starting point for investigations of workplace hazards, but the list I was reading that day on the outskirts of Chinandega told of health hazards far beyond anything I had ever encountered in the United States. Of the 125 workers, 31 had been treated for pesticide poisoning in a single month, a quarter of the entire airport workforce. From airplane mechanics and pilots to the laundry woman and night watchman, all had suffered an acute case of pesticide poisoning.

As I walked through the airport compound I began to understand how so many people in such varying occupations could have been exposed to high enough levels of pesticides to cause illness. I observed widespread contamination from pesticide spills from the daily mixing and airplane-loading process, which had built up to an incredible level over decades of careless and excessive pesticide use. The spilled chemicals had worked their way throughout the airport compound and into the surrounding drainage ditches, fields, and roadways. A follow-up study carried out by the Ministry of Health in the surrounding community gave further testimony to the extent of the problem. Forty percent of the children whose blood was sampled showed indications of pesticide exposure (McConnell et al. submitted). I began to realize that the scope of the pesticide problem in the cotton-growing region was almost beyond the comprehension of those unfamiliar with the conditions of Third World agriculture.

The problems that emerged from Central America's Golden Age represent a powerful indictment of the high-technology, yield-maximizing, agricultural development strategy pursued during this era. They also serve as a warning of the dangers inherent in the continued dependence on chemical-intensive agriculture in the developing world.

Historically, cotton-based development has led to impressive economic growth in many parts of the world. But cotton has frequently also generated a range of social problems. In many, if not all cases, cotton economies have been the source of increasing social inequity. The best-known, and perhaps not entirely atypical, example was the American South of the nineteenth century with its slave-based system of plantation agriculture (Fogel and Engerman 1974; Jones 1992; Wolf 1982).

Central America's cotton boom after World War II was also characterized by increasing economic wealth accompanying increasing impoverishment of large sectors of the rural populace. Although not based upon slavery, the Central American cotton economy nevertheless contributed to a heightening of the hardship and suffering of hundreds of thousands of rural workers, small farmers, and their families. For example, while regional gross domestic product rose 4.9 percent per annum from 1965 to 1975 (a considerable part of which resulted from the cotton boom), malnutrition was increasing among Central American children in all but Costa Rica (Brockett 1988:84).[1]

The declining level of caloric consumption was in part the result of the decrease in production of basic grains. With the takeoff of cotton production in Nicaragua, for example, land dedicated to cotton increased fourfold from 1952 to 1967, while basic grain production was cut by 50 percent (Weir and Shapiro 1981:36).[2] El Salvador and Guatemala went through similar transformations as cotton displaced traditional sources of subsistence and commercial production throughout the region. As cotton farming expanded, it displaced not only basic grain production and subsistence agriculture but also many of the people who had historically lived on the land. By the mid-1970s there were more than a half million peasants working as migrant laborers in the region (ICAITI 1977:190), many of whom had been legally or illegally evicted from the land to make room for cotton (Avery 1985).

The increasing gap between the rich and the impoverished rural majority invariably led to escalating social unrest, which made Central America a primary focus of international geopolitics by the early 1980s.

As a State Department analyst reported in a 1985 intelligence bulletin: "No other factor in Central America . . . seems to correlate so strongly with destabilization of governments as the expansion of cotton. . . . [T]he combination of displacement and increased disparity of incomes— or possibly even the prospects of the diverging paths of the traditional and export sectors of agriculture—apparently played a significant part in the susceptibility of Central American states to political destabilization" (Avery 1985:72–73). Discontent exploded into revolution, toppling the Somoza regime in Nicaragua in 1979 and fueling the ongoing conflicts between armed guerrilla movements and national governments in El Salvador and Guatemala. Central America slipped into a prolonged period of social and political crisis, while the regional economy stagnated.

The Ecology of Crisis

The social, political, and economic dimensions of the Central American crisis have been extensively analyzed,[3] as the 1980s became known as the Lost Decade. Cotton was generally recognized as a key factor in the emergence of this crisis. Also acknowledged, but less analyzed, was the role of the ecological disruption that accompanied cotton.[4] While the armed conflicts and economic recessions were occurring throughout the region, another crisis was building with less fanfare but with implications that were no less significant for the future of the region.

As noted in the previous chapter, pests were a primary obstacle to the successful development of cotton economies throughout history. With the advent of pesticides, cotton cultivation became a viable and appealing option for Central American development through the combined control of cotton pests and the disease vectors that plagued the lowland regions being opened up to cotton production. But once cotton expansion began, it quickly turned formerly diverse agricultural zones, as well as many previously undeveloped forest regions, into vast seas of monocultural production. Complex ecosystems of microorganisms, insects, plants, and animals existed before the advent of cotton. The elimination of many of these complexes was one of the first results, both intended and unintended, of cotton production.

Farmers used pesticides to transform existing ecosystems, creating a new ecology of cotton production.[5] Pesticides were constantly applied to assure that no pest populations developed as the cotton plants matured. Where mechanical harvesting was employed, cotton plants were again treated with paraquat and other defoliants prior to harvest to remove the leaves and thus ensure that the cotton fiber was not stained green as the machines stripped the bolls from the plants.[6]

Cotton producers, in keeping with the agronomic wisdom of the time, pursued a strategy of total pest eradication (Perkins 1982). No pest population, no matter how small, was tolerable for the risk-averse producers. Encouraged by chemical salespeople and agricultural technicians equally enamored of the chemical pest control paradigm, farmers commonly relied on calendar spraying, the application of chemicals at predetermined intervals throughout the season, to control real or anticipated pests (Table 3-1). These schedules were initially as much prophylactic as responsive to existing problems. When pest outbreaks occurred, even as calendar spraying continued, the cost of additional applications of

Table 3-1 Spray Schedule for Cotton-Pest Control in 1989 at Finca Jumay, Guatemala

Spray #	Date	Products
1	8/4	Methyl parathion (OP) + methamidophos (OP)
2	8/20	Methamidophos (OP) + cyhalothrin (SP)
3	8/27	Profenofos (OP) + cypermethrin (SP)
4	9/3	Methomyl (OP) + cypermethrin (SP)
5	9/9	IGR + cyhalothrin (SP) + methyl parathion (OP)
6	9/13	Methyl parathion (OP)
7	9/16	Cyfluthrin (SP)
8	9/22	Chlorofluazuron (IGR)
9	9/23	Methyl parathion (OP)
10	9/29	Methamidophos (OP) + methyl parathion (OP)
11	10/5	Profenofos (OP) + cyfluthrin (SP) + IGR
12	10/10	Methyl parathion (OP) + methamidophos (OP)
13	10/16	Methomidophos (OP) + IGR + methyl parathion (OP)
14	10/21	Methomyl (C) + cyhalothrin (SP) + methyl parathion (OP)
15	10/27	Cyfluthrin (SP) + methyl parathion (OP) + IGR
16	10/31	IGR + cyhalothrin (SP)
17	11/5	IGR + methamidophos (OP)
18	11/11	Cyhalothrin (SP) + methyl parathion (OP)
19	11/17	Cyfluthrin (SP) + methyl parathion (OP)
20	11/25	Cyfluthrin (SP) + methyl parathion (OP)
21	12/1	Cyfluthrin (SP) + methyl parathion (OP)
22	12/6	Methyl parathion (OP)
23	12/10	Methyl parathion + cyfluthrin (SP)

SOURCE: FAO 1990.

OP, organophosphate
SP, synthetic pyrethroid
IGR, insect growth regulator
C, carbamate

chemicals seemed minor compared to the considerable economic investment represented by the crop under cultivation, as well as the economic gains expected from the cotton harvest.

Although total eradication was initially effective in stimulating the cotton boom, it soon began to generate changes in the agroecosystem,[7] which ultimately brought about the very antithesis of pesticide-based expansion of the cotton sector. A series of interrelated processes eventually caused cotton production to plummet from its lofty perch as a crowning component of the Central American economies.

In the first decade of the twentieth century, researchers at Washington State College noted that lime-sulfur washes, traditionally used to kill scales that fed on apples, were becoming increasingly ineffective as the apple pests gradually became resistant to the effects of the pesticides. The finding remained a "little-known curiosity" for another half century (Hansen 1987:21). Researchers became keenly interested in the problem when it was discovered in 1954–1955 that the boll weevil was becoming resistant to a range of the new organochlorine pesticides used in cotton.

Pest resistance to pesticides, they soon concluded, was a predictable extension of the natural evolutionary development of insect species. Insect populations have resisted various stresses upon their survival for millions of years. In this sense they have been among the most adaptable creatures on the planet. Pesticides merely provided "a fast-forward demonstration of basic evolutionary theory" (Mathiessen 1992). With each pesticide application, the majority of the insects died off, but a few survived because of unusual genetic or behavioral characteristics. For example, a few insects may have had the capacity to detoxify the effects of the chemicals, or had an unusual integument that prevented the penetration of toxic molecules (Van den Bosch 1980). It has been argued that plant-feeding insects, the ones most likely to be pests, naturally develop the capacity to detoxify poisons because many plants generate chemicals that are thought to be defensive mechanisms against plant-eating insects (Krieger et al. 1971). Whatever the particular characteristic, these survivors were the result of a selection process set in motion by the pesticide technology. The survivors bred, and more and more of their progeny had similar resistant characteristics. Since some pest populations go through a number of generations in a single growing season, the evolution of more-resistant pests in farming regions often occurred at a relatively rapid rate. Similar patterns have been noted among non-insect pests, although to lesser degrees (Bull 1982:17). Weeds have been shown to become resistant to herbicides, and various fungi have become resistant to fungicides. Even rats have become resistant to warfarin, the most common form of rat-bait poison.

This process began to accelerate; pests that evolved resistance to a particular chemical over a number of years would become resistant to that chemical's replacement in a shorter period of time. Cross-resistance developed to the point that some pests became resistant to all the chemicals in a given family of pesticides, again at an accelerating rate. In some instances pests even developed resistance across different families of chemicals. Methyl parathion, for example, was shown to induce resistance to synthetic pyrethroids among pests in Central American cotton (FAO 1990b: 5). The new synthetic pyrethroids were not even introduced in Central America until 1980, yet within five to six years resistance to pyrethroids was already causing increasing rates of pyrethroid application (Table 3-2). By the late 1980s, pest resistance to a wide range of pesticides was being reported (Table 3-3) throughout the Central American cotton sector (Table 3-4).

Cotton production also led to another discovery, equally as disturbing as the resistance problem. In 1925–1926, Dr. J. Folsom found that calcium arsenate, the primary insecticide used for boll weevil control before World War II, was generating outbreaks of cotton aphids (*Aphis gossypii*) (Hansen 1987). Researchers found that the chemicals were killing a much wider range of insects than the target pests, which was leading to the emergence of new secondary pests.

Some of the insect species in the cotton fields were not plant feeders but were instead predacious or parasitic insects that fed on other organisms. By preying on insects such as aphids, these predators, or beneficials, kept insect pest populations low. Once the predators were eliminated or greatly reduced through the unanticipated effects of pesticides, the previously innocuous plant-feeding insects grew in numbers until they became economically threatening secondary pests. Or as one observer described the process, "Insects were promoted to pest status by pesticides" (Ehrlich 1992).

Two additional factors favored the development of pesticide-generated secondary pest problems. The first was the previously described ability of plant-feeding insects to develop resistance to pesticides. The beneficials, insofar as they were not plant eaters, were not as likely to develop a detoxifying capacity or resistance, at least not at the same rate as the plant-feeding insect populations. This contributed to the second factor. If the chemical applications decimated both pest and beneficial insect populations, the surviving pests still had an abundant food supply available in the form of cotton or other crops. The few beneficials that survived the chemical applications had a far more limited food supply in the few remaining pests. Thus the populations of beneficials were more likely to disappear, leaving the resistant plant-eating insects a safer environment in which to expand.

Table 3-2 Average Number of Pyrethroid Insecticides Applied for Control of Cotton Pests in Guatemala, Nicaragua, and El Salvador, 1989–1990

	Applications	Total products applied	Pyrethroids applied
Guatemala[a]	22	42	17
Nicaragua[b]	22	41	10
El Salvador[c]	22	30	8

SOURCE: Appel et al. 1991.
[a]Annual Report, Consejo Nacional del Algodon.
[b]Vargas et al. 1990.
[c]R. Daxl, personal communication.

Table 3-3 Resistance Factors for Adult Whitefly *Bemisia Tabaci*, 1987

Pesticide	Tiquisate, Guatemala	Gezira, Sudan	Adana, Turkey
Carbamate, Aldicarb	9	3	2
Organophosphates			
Methamidophos	400	660	300 +
Monocrotophos	290	234	300 +
Synthetic Pyrethroids			
Biphenthrin	460	3	8
Cyhalothrin	470	—	8
Cypermethrin	760	38	29
Deltamethrin	2000 +	30	208

SOURCE: FAO 1990.

Table 3-4 Reports of Suspected Resistance in the Cotton-Pest Complex of Central America by Farmers or Technical Officers, August 1990

	Boll Weevil	Bollworms	Leafworms	Whitefly
Guatemala	—	2	1	6
Nicaragua	—	5	1	2
El Salvador	—	—	2	1

SOURCE: FAO 1990a.

Pesticide resistance and the absence of natural enemies or checks on various pest populations combined to drive resistant and secondary pest problems. As one or both problems developed, pests became increasingly more threatening to the profitability of chemical-intensive farming. Farmers found that the gradual buildup of pests led to a qualitatively different level of problems, when pest resurgence occurred. One or more of the pest populations would explode in numbers much greater than those found in previous seasons. The result was a shift from a worrisome but relatively controllable problem to multiple and escalating problems that defied all control efforts. When single or multiple pest resurgence occurred, farmers were frequently faced with severe reduction in their harvests, at times losing entire crops.

The Pesticide Treadmill

All three of these related processes were driven by, and were contributing factors to, farmers' pest control practices. Farmers tended to respond to every new indication of pest problems by applying an increasing volume and variety of chemicals, in part because of the initial effectiveness of pesticide applications and in part because of heavy promotional efforts by proponents of chemical pest control. Given the dynamics behind the evolving pest problems, chemical pest control required a constant process of technological innovation to address the ever-changing needs of farmers. The ecology of chemical-based farming created a built-in demand for expanding the use of the technology. But pesticide innovation could not keep up with the evolutionary process, as pest populations evolved much faster than chemical technology (Figure 3-1). As one recent study concluded: "primary reliance on chemical control strategies over the long run will depend on a steady stream of new compounds with different modes of action that can also meet regulatory requirements and economic expectations—an unlikely prospect in many pest-control markets" (National Academy of Sciences 1989).

Compounding their problems was the tendency for chemical prices to increase, particularly after the early 1970s. At the same time crop yields did not continue to increase as they had initially. When pest resurgence became significant, producers in some regions saw significant declines in crop yields. Farmers found themselves on the "pesticide treadmill" (Van den Bosch 1980). Even those farmers who recognized the spiraling nature of their problem could not escape. Once the ecological disruption was under way, it could not be easily reversed. To stop spraying was to let the now pervasive pests wreak havoc, frequently meaning the farmer would lose much if not all of the existing crop, and possibly crops in

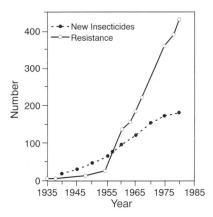

Figure 3-1 Cases of Arthropod Species Resistant to Insecticides (1935–1980) versus Cumulative Number of New Insecticides Introduced to the Market (1940–1980). SOURCE: Bull 1982.

one or more future seasons. Farmers already heavily in debt, either from previous seasons or from loans and investments in the current crop, were generally unable to sit idly by and wait for the agroecosystem to recover some balance. They also were unwilling or, more frequently, economically unable to alter their farming practices to allow them to escape the pesticide treadmill.

Pesticides, in effect, began to create the very problems they were touted to resolve, with the added twist that once they were introduced, it was significantly more difficult to reverse their negative effects. Population biologist Paul Ehrlich described the problems with the technology in unequivocal terms: "Like heroin, they promise paradise and deliver addiction" (Van den Bosch 1980: vii).

The cotton fields of the lower Rio Grande Valley of Texas were one of the earliest and most dramatic examples of the problems arising from this pesticide-generated ecological disruption. Secondary pest problems were the initial problem as the cotton bollworm, *Heliothis zea,* and the tobacco budworm, *Heliothis virescens,* began to cause economic damage to cotton in the 1950s, after years of the heavy use of organochlorine pesticides like DDT, BHC, toxaphene, dieldrin, and endrin had killed off the main predators of these pests (FAO 1990b: 12). The boll weevil also became resistant to a range of these pesticides within approximately fourteen years of their introduction, at which point cotton farmers switched to organophosphate pesticides, particularly methyl parathion.

Farmers began applying a mixture of DDT and methyl parathion to control both the cotton bollworm and the boll weevil. After another seven to eight years, the bollworm became resistant to DDT, and farmers responded by doubling and even quadrupling the dosage of methyl parathion. Only two to three years later the tobacco budworm developed resistance to organophosphates. Even with applications increasing to fifteen to twenty per season, considerable losses in yields occurred (FAO 1990b:12). Twenty-five years after the introduction of the first synthetic organic pesticides, several cotton pests had become resistant to one or more of the chemicals, with *H. virescens* resistant to all the available options.

The Texas cotton growers fell into a period of serious economic difficulty until the late 1970s, when the newest family of pesticides, the synthetic pyrethroids, was introduced, finally providing effective control of the budworm. Yet by 1985 the first signs of resistance to the new pesticides were being reported from the United States, Australia, Colombia, Thailand, and Turkey (Table 3-3). The findings of resistance to the new family of chemicals occurred in less than half the time it took the boll weevil to first develop resistance to the earlier organochlorine pesticides.

Cotton producers in Peru's Cañete Valley also entered a period of rapidly declining productivity during the 1950s. Resistance to pesticides and secondary pest problems continued to build in the Peruvian cotton fields until a resurgence of multiple pests reduced the 1956 cotton harvest to half of its previous level (Barducci 1972:424). Similar results in northeastern Mexico followed closely on the Texan and Peruvian experiences, with *H. virescens* virtually wiping out cotton production in the region by the end of the 1960s. In 1970, more than 700,000 acres of former cotton land were abandoned, as were cotton ginning facilities and entire communities dependent upon the cotton industry (Bull 1982:16). By the end of the 1960s, the ecological disruption caused by pesticide technology was fueling repeated crises from the southern United States through South America.

The Crisis in Central American Cotton Production

The experience of the Central American cotton-growing region is perhaps the most telling example of the range and depth of the problems this disruption engendered. Cotton growers stuck tenaciously to the chemical pest control paradigm, with few exceptions, throughout the postwar era.[8] As pest problems escalated, farmers consistently employed a wider range of products in increasing volume.

By the early 1960s, Central American cotton cultivation surpassed

200,000 hectares (Figure 2-2). The primary pest remained the boll weevil, which was controlled by ten to fifteen applications per season of the organochlorine pesticides DDT and toxaphene. But the boll weevil was gradually developing resistance to the organochlorines. At the same time, these chemicals were generating secondary pest problems such as leafworms (*Spodoptera exigua* and *S. frugiperda*), which began to cause significant economic losses along with *Heliothis zea* and *H. virescens*, the cotton aphid (*Aphis gossypii*), and the whitefly *Bemisia tabaci*. This in turn fueled further increases in pesticide use. By the end of the decade the application rates had doubled, with twenty or more applications of the organophosphate methyl parathion common. In extreme cases such as El Salvador, growers were reported to be making as many as fifty-six applications per season (Faber 1993).

The increasing pesticide use was both the cause and the consequence of the changing nature of the pest complex in Central American cotton. While the boll weevil continued to be a significant problem, along with the leafworm *Alabama argillacea*, newly resistant and secondary pests repeatedly became the source of explosive pest resurgence problems. The escalating use of organophosphates was largely responsible for the secondary pest problems, as the extremely toxic chemicals devastated populations of a wide range of insects and other creatures (ICAITI 1977: 162). By the mid-1960s, the bollworm, the cotton aphid, and the false pink bollworm (*Sacadodes pyralis*), had joined the boll weevil and the leafworm as significant pests (ICAITI 1977:29). At the end of the decade four additional pests—armyworms of the *Prodenia* and *Spodoptera* genera, the whitefly *Bemisia tabaci*, and the cabbage looper *Trichoplusia ni*—attacked cotton crops for the first time in Central America.

The whitefly in particular had devastating effects on the region's cotton production during the 1960s. First appearing in El Salvador in 1961–1962, it emerged in neighboring Honduras in 1964 and Nicaragua and Guatemala in 1965 (Smith and Reynolds 1972:395). This secondary pest resurgence, when combined with declining prices during the period, drove many cotton producers bankrupt (Williams 1986:35). Further heightening the effects of this problem was the migration of the whitefly into other crops such as beans, which caused additional hardship for subsistence producers in the region.

The proliferation of pest and pesticide problems led to several cycles of boom and bust in the Central American cotton economy. By the late 1960s, more than 120,000 hectares of cotton fields were out of production (Faber 1993). Nearly half the producers in El Salvador had been driven out of cotton farming. In Nicaragua, the increasing resistance of the boll weevil, along with secondary pests like the whitefly and bollworm, led to a 30 percent decline in cotton yields during the decade

(Conservation Foundation 1988:91). From 1965 to 1970, cotton production decreased at an annual average rate of 15.9 percent (Vaughn and
Leon 1977:812), even with the continued heavy reliance on pesticides.
An average of 99.2 liters of liquid pesticide and 18.7 kilograms of pesticide dust were applied during the 1966–1967 season (Bull 1982:21).

Cotton production began to recover in the 1970s, in spite of continuing pest problems. Higher market prices, combined with favorable
weather conditions that reduced pest problems, contributed to an expansion of cotton production and improvements in cotton yields. But
pesticide prices also began to rise, jumping dramatically after the first
of the global oil price hikes in 1973. In addition, pesticide use soon began its inexorable climb once again as farmers poured an ever greater
volume and variety of chemicals on their cotton fields. In Nicaragua,
insecticide use doubled from 1971–1972 to 1977–1978 (Swezey et al.
1986:31). Insecticide costs, as a percentage of production costs, declined slightly from 1971 through 1973 but then began to climb, reaching 30.7 percent by the end of the decade (Swezey et al. 1986:29). Guatemalan insecticide use reached 37 percent of production costs in the
same year (Williams 1986:210, n4).

The decade-long expansion of cotton production during the 1970s was
impressive, particularly after the decline in the latter half of the 1960s.
Cotton production reached an all-time high in the 1977–1978 season,
with 463,000 hectares harvested (Table 2-2). But the expansion of the
1970s was unsustainable. The 1978 harvest was the last hurrah for the
Central American cotton boom as it began a gradual and then accelerating decline into the 1980s, from which it has yet to recover.

The decline and eventual collapse of the cotton sector was the result
of a combination of factors, including those social and economic conditions that fueled the regional crisis. Increasing input costs and a weak-
ening in world market prices, caused in part by China's ascendancy as a
cotton-producing nation, further contributed to cotton's demise. The
Nicaraguan Revolution, which toppled the Somoza regime in 1979,
temporarily disrupted that nation's cotton production in 1979–1980.
The continued hostilities during the 1980s between the Sandinista regime and neighboring governments, with considerable provocation provided by the United States government and its proxy army, the contras,
caused labor shortages, equipment and input supply problems, and many
other difficulties that restricted Nicaraguan cotton farming throughout
the decade (Enriquez 1991). Cotton production also encountered major
obstacles in the rest of the region as civil war and social unrest increasingly disrupted the cotton sectors of El Salvador and Guatemala
throughout the 1980s.

The ecological disruption accompanying the continued dependence on pesticides was also an important factor in the decline of Central American cotton production. Pest problems and pesticide use fluctuated during the 1980s, but both remained at levels far above those at which cotton could remain viable. Recommended pesticide applications in Nicaragua in 1990 were still excessively high, at forty-six per season, including twenty-two applications of methyl parathion, six of other organophosphates, fifteen of various pyrethroids, and three of microbial pesticides (FAO 1990b:6). The boll weevil in Nicaragua was found to be thirty times more resistant than the boll weevil in the United States by 1987, because of Nicaragua's heavy reliance on methyl parathion over the previous twenty years (Swezey and Salamanca 1987). Pesticides accounted for over 50 percent of Nicaragua's cotton production costs. The high costs of pest control, combined with the declining international market price for cotton, drove down Nicaraguan cotton production from a region-leading 212,000 hectares in 1978 to only 35,000 hectares in 1990.

El Salvador followed a similar pattern, with cotton falling from 95,000 hectares in 1974 to only 10,000 hectares in 1990. Pesticides accounted for 45 percent of total production costs by the end of the decade (FAO 1990a). In Honduras, where cotton production was far less ambitious, cotton nevertheless fell from a high of 18,000 hectares in 1978 to 3,000 hectares by 1990. Guatemala appeared to be the only country in the region that maintained even a marginally profitable cotton sector into the 1990s. Although production fell from a high of 123,000 hectares in the late 1970s to only 46,000 hectares in 1990, the thirty-three remaining Guatemalan cotton producers continued to report profitable yields (FAO 1990a).

Nevertheless, the signs of impending collapse were present in Guatemala as well. Guatemala's cotton growers continued to make heavy applications of organophosphates and pyrethroids. A typical spray schedule for the 1989–1990 season included eighteen applications of methyl parathion, twelve of other organophosphates, fourteen of pyrethroids, and five of growth-regulating or microbial pesticides (FAO 1990b:8) (Table 3-1). Pesticide costs accounted for roughly 40 percent of total costs. In its regional evaluation of cotton production, the FAO concluded: "It is anticipated that insect resistance problems will increase in the near future associated with the overuse of pyrethroid insecticides which is likely to enhance the pest status of the whitefly to render the cotton unsaleable. In this case cotton production would cease in Guatemala" (FAO 1990b:16).

The FAO report went on to project that cotton prices would likely continue to decline in the 1990s and, with existing or anticipated prob-

lems related to pesticide-generated ecological disruptions and the failure of Central American private and public institutions to respond to
these problems, that cotton would virtually disappear from the region
by the year 2000.

The Environmental Consequences
of Pesticide-Intensive Cotton

Pesticides played both a direct and an indirect role in the environmental problems associated with the cotton boom. Indirectly, by fostering
the rise of intensive cotton cultivation, the technology contributed to
an array of environmental effects. The rapid clearing of Central America's forests, for example, was driven to a considerable degree by the cotton boom. In Guatemala, more than 153,000 hectares of forest were
cleared in the country's eight most important cotton-producing munici-
palities between 1950 and 1963 (Williams 1986:53). Although part of
the land was turned into pasture, the best tracts went to cotton. In El
Salvador, cotton accelerated the deforestation already under way along
the coastal plain. Honduras and Nicaragua followed similar patterns as
extensive new tracts were opened up for cotton farming.

While some of the deforestation was carried out to open land for cotton production, other areas were cleared to accommodate displaced
peasants and subsistence production because cotton was occupying the
most productive lands. These marginal, often hillside lands were quickly
depleted of their nutrients. Many trees surrounding the cotton fields
were also cut down to allow greater access for low-flying spray planes
as they swooped to within several feet of the tops of the cotton plants
to apply the pesticides. Once the trees were gone, dry-season winds
whipped through the cotton fields, carrying the loose, dry soil away.

The cotton-growing region soon became subject to heavy erosion as
seasonal torrential rains followed the dry winds and washed away un-
covered topsoil. The rains and dry-season winds annually carried away
an estimated sixteen to twenty tons of topsoil (per hectare) from the
cotton fields (ICAITI 1977:187). Central America soon achieved the dubious distinction of being the world leader in the percent of vegetated
land (24.1) suffering moderate to severe soil degradation (Figure 3-2). In
León, the once rich cotton-growing department on the coast of Nicaragua, 70 percent of the farmland suffered from moderate to strong erosion
by the mid-1980s (Castillo 1988:116). The erosion also contributed to
increasing siltation of the waterways, which led to reductions in aquatic
life. In 1982, heavy rains washed so much topsoil from the cotton fields
of Nicaragua that rivers and drainage canals in León and Chinandega

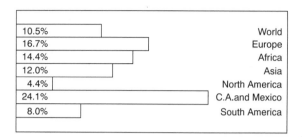

10.5%	World
16.7%	Europe
14.4%	Africa
12.0%	Asia
4.4%	North America
24.1%	C.A.and Mexico
8.0%	South America

Figure 3-2 Extensive Land Damage, by Share of Vegetated Land with Moderate to Severe Soil Degradation. SOURCE: International Soil Reference and Information Centre, cited in *Business Week* May 11, 1992.

became clogged with sediment, resulting in severe flooding and the destruction of numerous bridges and causing $20 million in damages (Faber 1991 : 33).

These effects can be described as indirect consequences of chemical technology, but the technology had much more direct effects on the environment as well. Ground and surface water sources throughout the cotton-growing region were gradually contaminated by the heavy use of pesticides. Rivers running through the flat coastal plains carried chemical residues to the coastal estuaries, where much of the aquatic life of the region could be found among the mangroves and lagoons. Indigenous communities in Nicaragua's cotton-growing region saw some of their primary food sources dwindle as shellfish and crayfish disappeared from the rivers and estuaries during the era of cotton expansion (D. Walker 1992). Nearby, Salvadoran shrimp harvests dropped by 50 percent as cotton plantations expanded on the watershed for the fishing grounds (FAO 1990a : 30).

Samples taken during the cotton era appeared to show that surface water was not retaining high levels of pesticide residues (Leonard 1987 : 147), possibly because of the shift from persistent organochlorine chemicals to the rapidly degrading organophosphates in the 1960s and 1970s. But the frequent reports of fish kills and the destruction of other aquatic life around the cotton fields indicated that heavy chemical runoff was indeed occurring. Some of this contamination was likely the result of chemicals trapped in the soil. Parathion, for example, degrades in less than a week from the surface of the cotton plants, but it takes three to six months to degrade in soil. Thus when heavy rains washed soil from the fields into the streams, major fish kills occurred as the toxic chemicals were released into the water.

More ominous were the findings of increasing levels of organochlorine contamination of the deep wells in the cotton region of Nicaragua during the 1980s, where chemicals found their way into aquifers hundreds of feet below the surface (Kline 1988). The fact that organochlorine use was drastically curtailed after the late 1970s suggests that these chemicals were still percolating down through soil and rock strata into community water supplies years after their use ended.

The combined direct and indirect environmental effects of pesticides have yet to be adequately evaluated. One United Nations study made rough estimates of the environmental and social damage caused by insecticide use in Nicaragua during the 1970s, placing the cost at $200 million annually (Falcon and Daxl 1977), compared to $141 million in income generated by cotton in Nicaragua's peak year of export earnings (Swezey et al. 1986). A comprehensive assessment that considered the broader range of direct and indirect effects would likely find the costs even higher. Further, a stratification of groups by the degree of pesticide impact would undoubtedly have shown that the poorer members of Central American society bore a much greater burden of the adverse effects of pesticides than did the rich. The health hazards of pesticides provide graphic evidence of how unequal this burden was.

The Public Health Consequences of Pesticide Use in Cotton

The health problems associated with pesticide use during Central America's cotton boom have also been widely reported, but again the problem has not been well analyzed. Numerous anecdotal accounts, including my own repeated personal experiences, suggest that pesticide poisoning is a far greater public health problem than was commonly acknowledged. The problem was not unique to Central America. Recognition of and response to pesticide-related health problems lagged far behind the responses to various other agriculturally-based development problems throughout the world during the cotton era, particularly those problems posing economic obstacles to development projects. Generally speaking, pesticide-related health problems were treated as a regrettable but unavoidable part of modernizing the agrarian sectors of the developing world (Wright 1990).

One indication of the inadequate attention given to the problem was the lack of reliable public health data on the severity of the problem. There was a complete lack of systematic reporting of pesticide poisonings and related health problems in Central America, and in most of the rest of the developing world as well. Government institutions largely ignored the problem, and private interests minimized or even concealed its scope and severity (Bull 1982; Cole 1988; ICAITI 1977).

On a global level, official estimates consistently understated the number of pesticide-related illnesses occurring annually (Levine 1985).

Early World Health Organization estimates placed the annual global rate at 500,000 in 1973 (WHO 1973). Fifteen years later the estimate was revised upward to 2 million to 3 million (WHO 1989).[9] A more sophisticated attempt at determining an illness rate estimated that as many as 25 million poisonings occurred annually, a rate that rivaled or surpassed many of the most serious illnesses in the developing world, placing pesticide-related illnesses at the top of the list of occupational hazards in many agrarian communities (Jeyaratnam 1990).

Most pesticides used in the early years of Central America's cotton boom were organochlorines (Table 3-5) with relatively low acute toxicity (Table 3-6). Small amounts of these pesticides, if spilled on the skin while mixing them with water or other liquids or loading them into airplanes or backpack sprayers, or if sprayed on field workers as planes passed overhead or as they applied the chemicals manually, usually did not result in acute symptoms. The low acute toxicity of the organochlorines became the standard degree of hazard that farm workers associated with the technology and that pesticide users became accustomed to during the initial decades of the cotton boom. But as the organochlorines lost their effectiveness in controlling the boll weevil and other pests, farmers began switching to far more toxic organophosphate pesticides. With this shift came an alarming increase in pesticide-related illnesses as extremely small amounts of the new compounds, when left on the skin for relatively short periods of time, led to the onset of acute pesticide poisoning. The most heavily used organophosphate, parathion (methyl and ethyl), was so acutely toxic that a single drop of the concentrate, if splashed in the eye, or the amount contained in a tablespoon, if left on the skin for several hours, could be fatal.[10]

Early indications of an impending health crisis appeared in Nicaragua during the 1952 cotton season. The German-based transnational chemical firm Bayer successfully tested methyl parathion in Nicaragua in February of the previous year (Swezey et al. 1986:9). Commercial application of the new organophosphate began with the fall spraying season as 1.2 million pounds of the pesticide were applied to 30,100 hectares of cotton. Although the resulting boll weevil control was considered impressive, the consequences in human health terms were nothing short of disastrous: several hundred poisonings, including dozens of fatalities, resulted when workers handled or were exposed to a chemical far more toxic than anything they had previously encountered. The insecticide was banned the following year by the Nicaragua Ministry of Agriculture, but cotton growers successfully pressured for its reintroduction in 1954. Methyl parathion has been used in the millions of pounds throughout Central America ever since. In the ensuing decades, this

Table 3.5 Insecticide Use in Central American Cotton by Major Chemical Group, 1974–1975

Country	Organochlorines volume (metric tons)	%	Organo-phosphates volume	%	Total volume	%
El Salvador	3,767.2	52.0[a]	3,292.8	48.0[a]	6,860.0	100
Guatemala	5,696.2	64.9[a]	2,378.7	27.1[a]	8,776.9	100
Honduras	58.5	33.3	117.1	66.7	175.6	100
Nicaragua	6,750.1	76.2	2,108.3	23.8	8,858.4	100
Total	16,072.0	67.0	7,896.9	33.0	23,968.9	100

SOURCE: ICAITI 1977:159.

[a]Based on a sample of 10–15 percent of planted area. All other figures relate to the total universe.

Table 3-6 Family and Acute Toxicity of Selected Pesticides

Chemical	Family	LD50[a]
Toxaphene[b]	Organochlorine	120 mg/kg rat oral 40 mg/kg cat oral 940 mg/kg rat dermal
DDT[c]	Organochlorine	113 mg/kg male rat oral >2510 mg/kg rat dermal
Parathion[c]	Organophosphate	13 mg/kg rat male oral 21 mg/kg rat male dermal
Methyl parathion[c]	Organophosphate	14 mg/kg rat male oral 64 mg/kg rat male dermal
Methamidophos[b]	Organophosphate	31 mg/kg male rat oral 84–94 mg/kg rat dermal
Carbofuran[d]	Carbamate	11 mg/kg rat oral 10,200 mg/kg rabbit dermal
Methomyl[d]	Carbamate	17–24 mg/kg rat male oral 5880 mg/kg rat male dermal

[a]LD50 is the lethal dose for 50 percent of the treated animals under strict laboratory conditions. This is determined by exposing laboratory animals to a predetermined amount of pesticide based on the animal's body weight. The amount of pesticide that causes a 50 percent death rate is the LD50. Pesticides with lower LD50s are more toxic. For example, it takes only 13 milligrams per kilogram of body weight of parathion to kill 50 percent of the male rats fed this amount of pesticide (oral route of exposure). In comparison, it takes 113 mg/kg of DDT to achieve the same results. Since human occupational exposure (the most common form of pesticide poisoning in Latin America) is most frequently dermal, it is important to note the dermal exposure LD50s. Some are quite high, indicating they are poorly absorbed through the skin; others, like parathion, are nearly as low as the oral LD50s, suggesting why this particular pesticide was the leading source of human poisonings for many years in many parts of the world.
[b]Hayes and Lawes 1991.
[c]Klaassen et al. 1986.
[d]Farm and Chemical Handbook 1992.

single pesticide accounted for up to 80 percent of the acute pesticide poisonings in Central America (Wolterding 1981).[11]

The range of reports, estimates, and anecdotal accounts suggests that the health problems became increasingly serious as cotton production expanded through the 1960s and 1970s. One early report placed pesticide poisonings in Nicaragua at 3,000 per year from 1962 to 1972 (Falcon and Smith 1973). The Ministry of Health in neighboring El Salvador reported approximately 1,000 cases annually that were treated in hospitals from 1966 through 1975, jumping to 2,500 by 1980 (FAO 1990b: 15). A regionwide survey documented 2,284 cases, with ten fatalities in 1975 (ICAITI 1977:91). Another regional study reported 19,930 cases from 1971 to 1976 (Mendes 1977). All those reports suffered from the same problems noted earlier. They commonly depended upon official government data, or at best included hospital or health clinic records. These sources so drastically underrepresented the actual rates of poisoning that they were almost meaningless.[12]

In contrast, anecdotal accounts from communities in the cotton-growing regions suggested significantly higher rates of poisoning. Reports of thirty to forty cases per day in individual rural health clinics during the two- to three-month peak spraying season were common.[13] As I noted in the beginning of this chapter, I encountered repeated examples of large-scale pesticide poisonings but saw infrequent official recognition of these cases beyond the local level.

The true dimensions of pesticide illness escaped the official estimates. Consequently it was common to find development planners and practitioners, government officials, and others expressing concern about the problem but concluding that realistically it did not compare with more-pressing health problems such as malaria or various infectious diseases. For example, I was confronted with such arguments when I proposed a regionwide pesticide health and safety program to one of the largest, U.S.-based international humanitarian organizations during a visit to New York in 1985. The agricultural programs officer for this organization asked, "For the sake of argument, how many people became ill from pesticides as compared to how many became ill from malaria?" He was challenging my contention that the problem warranted much higher priority than it was normally given by development institutions. Relying on official estimates, the technician believed that pesticide-related illness did not rival other health problems. Indeed, at that time I had little reliable data with which to respond.

To address that problem, I joined several U.S. and Canadian researchers and Nicaraguan government health workers to initiate a systematic effort both to document the actual scope of the problem and to devise better measures to reduce the rates of pesticide-related illnesses. A number of international organizations, led by CARE International, soon got involved and began working with the Nicaraguan Ministry of Health to improve the public health service reporting and record-keeping system in the department of León.[14] By the late 1980s the illness reporting system developed in León was the most elaborate and reliable system for documenting pesticide poisonings in Central America and among the best in the developing world (FAO 1990a; McConnell 1988).

With improvements in the record-keeping system, officially reported pesticide illnesses in León increased from fewer than 200 in 1983 to 1,266 by 1987 (Figure 3-3). The increase up to 1987 was considered more a product of improved reporting than an actual increase in the incidence of poisoning (Keifer and Pacheco 1991). However, the figure for 1987 and the decline in the following years were considered relatively accurate representations of the overall illness pattern. The decreasing number of poisonings was believed to be due in large part to the decline in cotton production as well as the overall decline of agricultural activity in the department.[15]

Once the record-keeping system had been strengthened, researchers began field surveys to determine the number of pesticide poisonings that did not reach public health clinics and thus did not appear in the reporting scheme. Relying on a self-reporting survey technique, cross-referenced with the public health service registry, researchers compared the number of cases of poisoning in several sample communities with the number of cases that were reported by the corresponding health centers.

The results gave striking testimony to the degree of underreporting and underestimation of pesticide-related health problems. Researchers

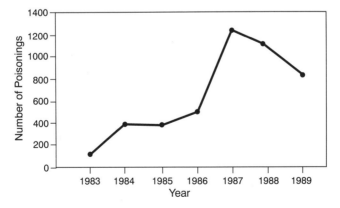

Figure 3-3 Reported Poisonings by Year, Department of León, Nicaragua. SOURCE: Keifer et al. 1989.

calculated that only 23 percent of the cases occurring in the countryside appeared in the official illness reports, leading to a revised estimate of 4,777 to 10,343 poisonings for 1989 among a rural population of approximately 300,000 in the department of León (Keifer and Pacheco 1991). This revised illness rate surpassed the reported rate of malaria in the department and made pesticide poisoning by far the leading cause of work-related illness and injury.

Acute pesticide poisonings became one of the most serious worker and public health problems in the Central American cotton-growing regions, but other health problems, not so immediately obvious, were also developing. Although long-term effects of pesticide exposure were not well recognized and were far less understood than the acute health problems, several indicators of the potential for such problems are sufficient to suggest the long-term hazards facing Central Americans exposed to pesticides during the cotton era.

The heavy volume of organochlorines applied in the cotton fields over several decades resulted in a significant buildup of the persistent chemicals in the environment and food chain. These low-polarity compounds were relatively insoluble in water and tended to accumulate in the fatty tissues of animals, from which they were slow to excrete. Thus they began to concentrate in the fat cells of creatures at the upper end of the food chain, most notably among humans living in and around the cotton-growing zones. A study conducted in 1971 found levels of DDT and metabolite residues in human milk samples (high in fat content) from Guatemalan women at 12.2 parts per million, 250 times the maximum tolerance level of 0.05 ppm set by WHO for DDT in cow's milk (FAO 1990b:14). Comparable levels of DDT were found in samples from El Salvador, and high levels of toxaphene (a pesticide similar to DDT) were found in samples from Nicaragua. Samples of human milk from women living in León in the mid-1970s averaged 2.29 ppm of DDT and its metabolites, eleven times higher than previously found in cow's milk samples from the region (Swezey et al. 1986:29). Women in the city of León, who presumably consumed meat and dairy products contaminated with the pesticide, had average breast-milk samples of 2.12 ppm, only slightly lower than the rural cohort. These levels were 42 to 45 times higher than WHO's maximum.

Human tissue samples taken in 1980 showed Nicaraguans to have some of the highest DDT burdens in the world: 97 ppm, eleven times the levels found in a cross-cultural and cross-socioeconomic strata study in South Florida (ICAITI 1977:129) and sixteen times the global average (Swezey et al. 1986). Following the ban of DDT in Guatemala in 1979, DDT levels in human breast-milk samples dropped 36 percent by 1982 (FAO 1990b:14). Meanwhile, El Salvador used more than 3.5 million pounds of DDT in 1979.

Organochlorines have long been suspected as human cancer-causing agents, as well as sources of various other long-term health effects.[16] Although the degree of risk posed by the high levels of DDT found in Central Americans remains unknown, the results of one recent study suggest there is ample cause for serious concern. A study of women in New York City found a fourfold increase in the risk of breast cancer among women with relatively high levels (19.1 parts per billion) of DDE (the metabolite produced by the breakdown of DDT in the human body) in blood serum, compared with women with lower levels (2 ppb) (Wolff et al. 1993). Breast cancer is one of the most frequent killers of women in the United States, and it appears to have been on the rise in recent years, leading the authors of the study to conclude that "the implications [of this study] are far-reaching for public health intervention worldwide" (Wolff et al. 1993:648).

Indeed, the implications for Central American women may be of even greater significance. A study of DDE levels in the blood serum of Salvadoran women found average levels of 101 ppb (Calderon et al. 1981), over five times the levels associated with elevated breast cancer risks in the U.S. population, suggesting that Central American women are likely to be facing risks even greater than those causing such concern among the U.S. medical community.

The Case of Chlordimeform

While the long-term consequences of organochlorine exposure remained the subject of debate among scientists, policymakers, and others, there were examples of long-term hazards from pesticides that were less debatable. Chlordimeform was one case that suggested the potential for long-term risks that accompanied pesticide use in the cotton fields of Central America.

Chlordimeform was introduced in 1966 and was immediately heralded as an important advance in chemical pest control technology. The pesticide acted as an ovicide, controlling pests while still in the egg or larval stage. The cotton bollworm, one of the most problematic cotton pests, was the primary target of the new chemical, but it was also effective against a range of other insects.

The new pesticide was considered an improvement over organophosphates because it had a comparatively lower acute toxicity. It was far less persistent than the organochlorines and thus posed reduced environmental hazards. It was also effective at very small doses and thus required low application rates. It quickly replaced the more toxic and persistent chemicals, and both chemical salespeople and agricultural technicians began touting chlordimeform as a useful component of integrated pest management (IPM) strategies incorporating both chemical and nonchemical techniques (ICAITI 1977 : 184).

The new pesticide became widely used in Central America, not only on cotton but on fruits, vegetables, and basic grains as well. Then in 1976, Japanese researchers found chlordimeform to be a potent cancer-causing agent in studies on laboratory mice. The primary manufacturers, Ciba Geigy and Schering, voluntarily withdrew the product from the market in response to the new cancer data. But following further tests, the companies reintroduced the chemical in 1978 with data supporting the contention that the product could be used safely.

By 1980 a million pounds of chlordimeform were being sold in the U.S. annually (*Wall Street Journal* Jan. 22, 1987). By the mid-1980s the product represented roughly 5 percent of Ciba Geigy's $3.6 billion annual global sales of pesticides (*Wall Street Journal* Nov. 9, 1987), as Ciba Geigy soon became the world leader in pesticide sales (Table 3-7).

Ciba Geigy and Schering's claims for their product's safety were based on a series of recommendations concerning chlordimeform's use. The companies recommended that it be used only on cotton and not on food crops; that only trained and well-supervised workers mix, load, and apply the chemical; that it be mixed and loaded only with closed-system loading equipment; that it be applied only by airplane, thus avoiding the higher exposure rates commonly associated with backpack application equipment; and that regular monitoring, in the form of urine sampling, be conducted for workers exposed to the chemical.

But the reality of the developing world soon came into conflict with

Table 3-7 Top Agrochemical Companies, Based on 1990 Sales

1.	Ciba Geigy	11.	Cyanamid
2.	ICI	12.	Schering
3.	Bayer	12.	Sandoz
4.	DuPont	14.	Kumiai
5.	Rhone-Poulenc	15.	FMC
6.	Monsanto	16.	Rohm and Haas
7.	Dow Elanco	17.	Sankyo
8.	Hoechst	18.	Nihon Nohyaku
9.	BASF	19.	Takeda
10.	Shell	20.	Hokko

SOURCE: Knirsch 1991.

the chemical companies' recommendations. Company monitoring programs in Central America and elsewhere found that supervision and training were not effective in controlling the use of the chemical, and safety equipment was not being properly used or maintained. In many instances effective protective measures were simply not feasible (see further discussion in Chapter 7).

Urine samples from exposed workers provided graphic evidence of the risks of pesticide use even under the most advanced conditions of supervision and control in the developing world. Roughly one third of the workers exposed to chlordimeform in Guatemala and Nicaragua during the mid to late 1980s were found to have unacceptably high levels of the cancer-causing agent in their urine. Sampling results from León, Nicaragua, in 1986 were indicative. Of the 106 workers monitored, 42 (39.62 percent) had satisfactory levels of chlordimeform in their urine of 0 to 0.5 ppm. Eighteen (16.98 percent) had unsatisfactory levels ranging from 0.51 to 1.0 ppm, and 46 (43.40 percent) had bad levels greater than 1.0 ppm (Pacheco 1987). Within this latter group were workers who had levels in excess of 5 ppm (13, or 12.26 percent of the total group), including one at 55.6 ppm.

Although a considerable percentage of the workers being monitored throughout Central America fell into categories of unacceptable exposure as defined by the companies, the manufacturers nevertheless argued that the exposure levels were within an acceptable range of hazards, and they continued to market the pesticide. Meanwhile, other problems were appearing. In spite of recommendations to the contrary, chlordimeform continued to be used in a wide range of food crops in Central America. Chlordimeform was commonly applied to basic grains (corn and beans), vegetables, and soybeans in Nicaragua (personal communication, Alvaro Fiallos, May 14, 1987).

In addition, pests were rapidly becoming resistant to the chemical, as indicated by the increasing application rates for cotton. According to Alvaro Fiallos, director of the Nicaraguan Cotton Experiment Station, chlordimeform application rates had gone from 3 per season, at a dosage of 250 to 300 cc per manzana (0.705 hectare), to 6 applications at 400 cc per manzana by 1978. By the 1986–1987 cotton cycle, Fiallos's investigators had found that chlordimeform was being applied on average 16.3 times per season at 600 cc to 1 liter per manzana (personal communication, Fiallos, May 14, 1987).

Then in early 1987, the medical department of the German chemical manufacturer Hoechst found that 8 workers in a cohort of 335 employees who had been involved in the production of 5-chloro-o-toluidine (5-COT) had developed bladder cancer. The chemical was an intermediate step in the manufacture of chlordimeform. The disease's incidence among those workers (2 of whom had died), was 73 times higher than normally expected for this rare form of cancer. Unfortunately for Central American farmers and farm workers, once chlordimeform is absorbed into the human body, it is metabolized back into 5-COT, which means any pesticide users who absorbed chlordimeform were exposed to this cancer-causing, intermediate compound as well.

Researchers determined that the mean exposure period to 5-COT for the eight manufacturing workers had been 11.4 years, and the latency period (the time between the beginning of exposure and the discovery of tumors) was 26 years. When the new findings were matched with the exposure data being collected in Central America and elsewhere, Ciba Geigy concluded it could no longer argue that the risks for exposed workers were acceptable, and the company voluntarily withdrew the chemical from the Central American market. Curiously, in a meeting I attended at the Nicaraguan Cotton Experiment Station in May 1987, Schering representatives argued that further study was necessary before regulatory restrictions were warranted. The company lobbied for the continued use of chlordimeform in Central America for one or more additional seasons, but Nicaraguan authorities rejected Schering's appeal and suspended the registration of chlordimeform in the spring of 1987.

The consequences of the use of this one pesticide for Central Americans and other Third World farmers and farm workers may not appear for decades. Given the twenty-six-year latency identified in the Hoechst case, the first cases of cancer can be expected to appear soon. How many people will eventually fall victim to chlordimeform is difficult to estimate. There were undoubtedly hundreds of thousands of Third World farmers and farm workers who received significant exposure to chlordimeform over the more than two decades it was in use.

Those who fell into the upper range of that exposure can be considered to have a very high risk of developing cancer. Calculations for this high-exposure cohort led the California Department of Health Services to conclude that a "realistic assumption," based on twenty years of working with chlordimeform (urine excretion rate of 30 ppm/day) five days a week during three months of each year, was a cancer rate of 1 per 1,000 (Hooper 1982). That rate is one hundred to one thousand times greater than the standard cancer risk factors considered acceptable by the EPA for pesticide exposure among the general population.

The story of chlordimeform may not be representative of all pesticides, but it suggests that potentially major public health costs associated with heavy pesticide use during the cotton era remain. Further, it suggests that the consequences of decades of heavy and relatively indiscriminate pesticide use still may not have appeared or been recognized.

The Resurgence of Malaria

Finally, another serious health problem evolved with the use of pesticides; one study concluded that it was "perhaps the most significant economic consequence of pesticide use in cotton" (ICAITI 1977:150). Just as the boll weevil and other pests had become resistant to pesticides over time and generated increasing crop losses, so too did the malaria vector *Anopheles albimanus* become resistant to the same chemicals, leading to a resurgence in the incidence of this disease and an array of climbing economic costs.

Control of mosquitoes and other vectors of disease had been enormously successful throughout the world after the introduction of DDT and other chemicals. Latin America was the most successful region in the world in controlling malaria. By 1970, deaths from the disease had all but disappeared (Clyde 1987). But in Central America, as elsewhere, this success began to weaken as the decade progressed. One reason was the heavy environmental contamination caused by pesticide residues in the areas surrounding the cotton fields. The numerous canals that bordered the fields, created to provide drainage during the rainy season, accumulated slow-moving water heavily contaminated with chemical residues. These canals provided an ideal environment for the selection process described earlier. In this case, succeeding generations of genetically or otherwise protected larvae became ever more resistant to pesticides. The resistant mosquitoes were increasingly difficult to control by the conventional methods of spraying swamps and other breeding grounds or the walls of dwellings where mosquitoes rested while awaiting the opportunity to feed. Pesticide resistance in the malaria vector fueled a resurgence in the disease reported in the cotton-growing zones of Central America.

In the late 1960s to early 1970s, vector resistance began reversing the gains that had been made since the end of World War II in malaria control. Reported illnesses jumped in El Salvador from 25,300 in 1969 to 83,300 in 1976 (Bull 1982:30). Similarly, in Honduras the figures rose from 8,800 in 1973 to 48,800 in 1976, and in Nicaragua from 4,200 in 1973 to 26,200 in 1976. A study of several Guatemalan communities during this period concluded that a statistically significant increase in the rate of malaria (0.136 cases per 1,000 population) occurred with every 1 percent increase in the area planted in cotton, as a consequence of heavy pesticide use (ICAITI 1977:129).

Variations in vector control strategies, including the shift to new chemicals, appeared to curb temporarily the resistance problems and the increases in malaria. But by the end of the 1970s malaria was on another upswing, and in the 1980s it once again became a scourge of the developing world. The Central American regional rate in 1980 was 65.7 cases per 1,000 population, much higher than the 1972 rate of 39.2 per 1,000 (Faber 1992). In Guatemala, rates were eleven times higher in 1981–1983 than a decade earlier (Barry 1987:100). Nicaragua's rates were four times higher by 1982 than they had been a decade earlier (Swezey et al. 1986:30), and Costa Rica reported a fourfold increase from 1981 to 1987 (Thrupp 1988:20). The Central American regional incidence was estimated at 200,000 cases annually by the late 1980s (Barry 1987:100), and seventeen countries in Latin America were seriously affected by the disease, with more than two million cases reported annually (Clyde 1987).

Conclusion

Pesticides contributed mightily to the increase in wealth and productivity in Central America, but so too did they contribute to the increase in misery in the region. Hidden within the ecological transformations that allowed cotton farming to thrive was an ecological crisis that played a significant role in the demise of the cotton sector. Degraded land and water, escalating pest problems, resurgence of malaria and other diseases, all combined with high rates of pesticide poisoning to seriously affect the well-being of rural society in the cotton-growing region. Even though cotton began to disappear as Central America fell into the Lost Decade of the 1980s, the ultimate toll of human and environmental destruction remains unknown because the long-term damage to public health and the environment is still so poorly understood.

The consequences of the failure to appreciate these pesticide problems become clear in the following analysis of the measures that have been taken by development planners and development institutions since the onset of the crisis at the end of the 1970s. Pesticides again have become a central feature of the development efforts initiated by Central American and Caribbean countries seeking relief from economic stagnation and social turmoil. Although the consequences of current development policies are less clear than those of the cotton era, the similarities between the previous and current strategies should be apparent, leading to the obvious question: Have development planners, in their effort to resolve the crisis of the 1980s, again placed the countries of the developing world on a collision course with ecological crisis and all its social and economic consequences?

4

Addressing the Crisis through Nontraditional Agriculture

During the mid-1980s I returned from Nicaragua to the United States on a regular basis. On several occasions I made presentations to university, church, and community groups, as well as to people at USAID and to several congressional staffs in Washington, D.C. On one occasion, I even made a presentation about pesticide problems and options for their resolution at the U.S. Department of State. It was not uncommon, while presenting my findings, to be challenged by industry or government representatives who asserted that much of my evidence of pesticide problems was from Nicaragua, which they argued was not representative of other countries and other regions of the Third World.

My presentation at the U.S. Department of State was indicative of these critiques. A high-level executive of the National Agricultural Chemical Association (NACA), who had been invited by USAID to attend my presentation, challenged the representativeness of the Nicaragua case by arguing that such conditions were more a reflection of conditions under communist regimes around the world than an indication of pesticide-related problems found in other countries.

I responded that although some efforts of the Nicaraguan government could certainly have been described as inept, the commitment it made during that period represented considerable human and material resources at a time when the country had precious little to spare. I doubted any other country in the region could match the resources committed by the Nicaraguans to addressing the health problems caused by pesticides or to research and development of alternative pest control strategies (see Chapter 6).

Still, I was willing to accept that the extreme conditions I witnessed in Nicaragua would one day disappear as the vestiges of traditional plantation agriculture gave way to more modern forms of social and economic organization in agricultural production. I certainly found it reasonable to assume that with the decline of cotton, the scope of pesticide problems would likely decline as well, not only in Nicaragua but also throughout Latin American agriculture. Then, in early 1989, I was hired as a consultant by USAID to investigate the sources of a series of pesticide problems emerging in the new nontraditional agricultural crops in the Dominican Republic. During 1989 and 1990, I conducted two one-month investigations in the Dominican Republic and an additional one-month study, financed by USAID, of similar problems in Guatemala. I concluded that far from disappearing, pesticide problems persisted and were increasing in some parts of Latin America. Further, I believed that U.S. development policy was playing an important role in perpetuating these problems.

Such conclusions were not well received within USAID or by the private-sector consultants largely responsible for many of the USAID projects. So over the ensuing four years I investigated pesticide use in nontraditional agriculture throughout Central America and in the Caribbean, financed by various research grants. The disconcerting results of this research, presented in the following two chapters, suggest that Central America is in many ways as far today from a resolution of the pesticide problem as it was at the height of the cotton era.

Managing the Crisis

During the early 1980s U.S. development planners began formulating various measures to extract the region from the grip of the escalating economic and sociopolitical crisis that became the basis for the Lost Decade. Ambitious proposals involving multibillion-dollar development schemes emerged from the inner circles of the Reagan Administration's foreign-policy apparatus, accompanied by boldly optimistic promises for a new and more prosperous partnership between the north and south.

Given the still-growing dimensions of the regional crisis during this period, one might expect that solutions to the ecological crisis described in the previous chapter, and particularly the pesticide problems so central to its development, would have received a relatively lower priority in the emerging proposals than those measures promising immediate relief from the economic, social, and political strife. But even in the context of the most severe economic crisis in the region's modern history, it is hard to understand how the ecological crisis in cotton came to be so totally ignored in the strategies for reactivation and reconstruction of the regional economies.[1]

Recognition of ecological problems was indeed largely missing from the primary development policies and programs initiated in response to the regional crisis. A few conservation measures were incorporated into existing or new development projects, and several debt-for-nature swaps reflect an increasing interest in curbing at least some of the ecologically destructive effects of the preceding development strategies. But the thrust of the strategy for regional recovery during the 1980s looked surprisingly similar to the strategy of the previous era, based on short-term growth and agricultural exports.

Unfortunately, the failure to alter significantly the traditional path of regional development in the 1980s has re-created some of the conditions that led to the pesticide-driven ecological crisis in the cotton sector. In spite of increasing evidence that the Golden Age's agro-export model is unsustainable, development planners appear to have looked backward while designing the future, giving latter-day testimony to the wisdom of the nineteenth-century French writer Alphonse Karr, who observed, "Plus ça change, plus c'est la même chose."[2]

The Reagan Administration's response to the regional crisis was first and foremost a military one, which by 1981 included the organizing of the contra army to subvert the Sandinista-led Nicaraguan Revolution, the provision of U.S. military advisors to the Salvadoran military to combat the increasingly successful Faribundo Martí National Liberation Front, and preparations for U.S. military and training bases in Honduras (Williams 1986). By 1985 the United States was spending half a billion dollars annually on military assistance to Central America.

Recognizing the limits of an exclusively military strategy, President Reagan proposed a sweeping economic development program, the Caribbean Basin Initiative (CBI), in February 1982, which was passed into law in August of the following year. The CBI created an unwieldy union of Central American and Caribbean nations, essentially for geopolitical reasons, and proposed the reactivation of export-led development throughout the region.[3] The CBI called for significant incentives to foreign investment in the regional economies and promised improved regional access to the U.S. markets for Caribbean Basin exports.

The U.S. economy was also in a recession during this period, and Congress was initially reluctant to approve more than relatively modest funding for the administration's program. So President Reagan commissioned a bipartisan panel of scholars, business people, development planners and practitioners, and legislators to assess the dimensions of the regional crisis and to make recommendations for its resolution. The commission's report of January 1984 (Kissinger 1984) remains the most comprehensive statement of U.S. strategy toward the Caribbean Basin formulated in the last decade. It essentially argues that the Alliance for Progress was a success in promoting economic development and political stability in the region, until a global economic crisis undermined the gains of the 1960s and 1970s. A primary goal established by the commission was the re-creation of the precrisis growth rates in the region. To achieve renewed economic success, the commission proposed the infusion of $24 billion over seven years, with $10 billion to $12 billion coming from the United States and the rest of the support divided between multilateral lending institutions and private-sector investment (Kissinger 1984).

In keeping with the Reagan (and subsequently Bush) Administration's vision of development priorities, government regulation and spending were seen as primary obstacles to viable economic development. The report called for the removal of various government controls on investment and trade and the reduction of public sector involvement in the economy more generally. Similarly, the report lauded the private sector as the source of previous successes and the appropriate engine of future development. The social and political dimensions of the regional crisis were attributed to the combined effects of the global economic crisis, a range of mistaken and inefficient or corrupt government policies in the region, and that traditional article of faith of U.S. foreign policy, the influence of outside subversive elements (i.e., Cuba and the Soviet Union). Subsequent U.S. development measures in the region built upon the commission's analysis and recommendations.

Although there was significant debate over the intentions and implications of the administration's strategy, there was almost universal agreement that one promising area of development for the Caribbean Basin was the diversification of the agricultural export base of the regional economies. When the global economy fell into recession at the end of the 1970s, the narrow base of the Caribbean Basin economies began to crumble. Demand and prices declined for the now-traditional agricultural exports of cotton, cattle, and sugar, as well as the still more traditional exports of coffee and bananas. At the same time, the prices of the array of manufactured consumer and capital goods imported from the developed world increased, leading the region into economic stagnation and crisis.

Diversification of the agricultural export base was seen as the fastest way to reactivate economic development and generate at least a portion of the capital necessary for regional reconstruction. Calls for agricultural diversification came not only from the administration but also from the opposing Democratic side of Congress through the Sanford Commission Report—named after Senator Terry Sanford, who was the principal catalyst for the commission's work (Sanford 1989), as well as from a range of more liberal (Bulmer-Thomas 1987) and radical (Fagen 1987; Gorostiaga and Marchetti 1988) proposals.

Diversification, as it emerged from the CBI and related projects sponsored by the United States, involved the promotion of a wide range of new "nontraditional" export crops. Nontraditionals were commodities that had not previously been central in a country's export profile. The new crops included cantaloupes, pineapples, strawberries, broccoli, snow peas, and dozens of other fresh and frozen fruits and vegetables destined primarily for U.S. or European markets. By diversifying into this broader range of crops, it was argued, the regional economies would be insulated from price and demand fluctuations in the global economy.[4]

The hope for economic growth appeared to be well founded, as the

Table 4-1 Nontraditional Exports to the United States from Selected Countries, 1983–1991 (millions of current U.S. dollars)

	1983	1984	1985	1986	1987	1988	1989	1990	1991 (est.)	Average annual growth rate 1983–1991
Central America										
Costa Rica	14.5	21.5	23.6	33.7	41.8	55.0	81.0	98.5	104.9	28.0%
El Salvador	2.4	3.2	3.9	4.9	6.8	5.0	5.6	6.3	7.0	14.6%
Guatemala	16.0	21.4	22.1	29.5	36.6	37.6	47.9	53.8	53.4	16.2%
Honduras	12.3	15.5	18.5	17.3	28.8	19.9	23.5	23.8	26.2	9.9%
Caribbean										
Dominican Republic	33.7	38.9	42.0	45.3	40.9	43.7	46.9	47.8	51.6	5.5%
Jamaica	4.8	4.9	5.5	5.4	5.9	5.1	6.4	6.5	7.8	6.3%
% change for total CBI	31.7		16.8	17.4	16.6	1.0	19.7	13.4	6.4	15.0%

SOURCE: U.S. Department of Commerce, "Imports for Consumption, Customs Value," compiled by USAID, Washington, D.C.

nontraditional sector experienced impressive growth rates during the 1980s. For example, in the early to mid-1980s, the Dominican Republic became the showcase for the CBI, with nontraditional agricultural exports expanding at an average annual rate of 13 percent (Mathieson 1988) and reaching $45.3 million by 1986 (Table 4-1). While the value of nontraditional agricultural exports remained well below traditional sectors of the Dominican economy, industry sources projected major growth, to exceed $150 million annually by 1992, with the successful implementation of new cut-flower and pineapple projects (Murray et al. 1989). That prediction, decidedly optimistic in hindsight, would have rivaled the Dominican Republic's traditional mainstay, sugar.

In Costa Rica, nontraditional exports (agricultural and industrial)[5] destined for markets outside the region grew at an annual rate of 28 percent from 1983 through 1989, rising from $128 million to $566 million, at which point nontraditionals represented 42 percent of total Costa Rican exports (Zuvekas 1992). Nontraditional agricultural exports to the United States alone reached nearly $100 million by 1990 (Table 4-1). Nontraditional agricultural exports throughout the Caribbean Basin grew 15 percent annually from 1983 through 1991, as the promotion of nontraditional exports and agricultural diversification appeared to be a dynamic and promising course of development.

Pesticides and Nontraditional Agriculture

Unlike the previous wave of agricultural diversification, the new nontraditionals involved a wide range of crops, each dependent upon different agroecological, production, and marketing systems. Many were crops that had traditionally been grown in more temperate climates, like broccoli, snow peas, asparagus, and strawberries (Table 4-2). When introduced into the more tropical regions like Central America and the Caribbean, these crops tended to encounter increasing pest problems. Pests are more generally a problem in tropical climates than in temperate climates, even for many native crops.

Pest problems also arose from the increasingly monocultural nature of many of the growing regions for the new crops. As more and more land was shifted to crops that generate high income, much of the local diversity that previously helped to provide some check on the growth of pest populations disappeared.[6] Growers relied on pesticides to replace the dwindling ecological controls. In addition, fresh fruits and vegetables destined for U.S., European, or Japanese markets were subject to stringent cosmetic and grading standards imposed either by producer associations in the developed world or in response to consumer de-

Table 4-2 Commodity Composition of
Nontraditional Exports from Central America, 1989

	Millions of US$	% of total
Fresh fruits	102.5	34.8
Pineapples	51.0	17.3
Melons	31.9	10.8
Fresh vegetables	28.3	9.6
Snow peas	8.2	2.8
Broccoli	4.1	1.4
Chayote squash	5.2	1.8
Root crops	16.8	5.7
Yucca	8.0	2.7
Flowers, plants, etc.	61.2	20.8
Others	47.2	16.0
Sesame seed	27.5	9.3
Tobacco	21.7	7.4
African palm oil	7.0	2.4
Cocoa	5.7	1.9
Plantain	5.8	2.0
Total	315.3	100.0

SOURCE: Kaimowitz 1991.

mands. These quality standards placed even greater pressure on producers to use a wide range of pesticides in order not only to maintain crop yields but also to assure produce appearance, shape, color, and size.

Farmer access to pesticides had not changed appreciably since the era of the cotton boom. The pesticide industry continued to maintain an effective and sophisticated system of pesticide promotion and distribution throughout the region. Government controls of pesticide importation, distribution, and use had also not changed significantly, in spite of the adoption of various pesticide laws in the 1970s and 1980s. Although pesticide registration standards were relatively good, application and enforcement of these and other laws were extremely weak (Harman 1990). In the Dominican Republic, for example, pesticides began to be registered at a rapid rate during the late 1970s and into the 1980s, increasing from an estimated total of twelve to fifteen products in the mid-1970s to more than nine hundred products registered by 1989 (Murray et al. 1989:9). The Dominican government registration list, similar to the lists for most Central American countries during the 1980s, included pesticides that had been banned, never registered, or severely restricted in the United States. Nontraditional farmers in the region continued to have easy access to many of these products.

The control of pesticides remained weak in part because of the economic crisis and the range of policies imposed by international lending institutions and USAID to spur economic growth. The "structural adjustment" measures in particular, which forced significant reduction in public-sector revenues, led to a declining state capacity to maintain even minimal regulatory and social services (Conroy et al. forthcoming). Ministries of agriculture found themselves increasingly unable to maintain sufficient numbers of inspectors, technicians, and extension agents in the field as vehicles, equipment, and other government infrastructural supports disappeared. For example, the Honduran Secretaría de Recursos Naturales, responsible for both agricultural and environmental regulation, saw its operating budget reduced by 50 percent during the 1980s (USAID 1990). In Costa Rica, only 18 percent of the 941 firms that reportedly handle agrochemicals (i.e., pesticide distributors, formulators, and manufacturers) were registered with the government agencies responsible for regulating the use of hazardous substances, partly because of the shortage of government inspectors (*Agence France-Presse* July 19, 1992).

Pesticide use tended to decrease with the decline of cotton in the 1980s and the deepening of the regional crisis. In Guatemala, for example, import of pesticide products dropped from 14,723,188 kilograms in 1982 to 5,074,954 kilograms in 1985 (Campos 1986: Table 4), as cotton hectarage declined by 50 percent during the same period. In Nicaragua the drop in pesticide imports was due not only to the reduction of cotton hectarage but also to the economic crisis and the war with the U.S.-backed contra rebels, as well as the absence of a growing nontraditional agricultural sector (Appel et al. 1991) (Table 4-3).[7]

Yet pesticide use did not decline uniformly throughout the region. Costa Rica was the leader in Central American nontraditional agricultural growth throughout the 1980s and had never cultivated more than a few thousand hectares of cotton. Consequently, even though declining cotton production lowered pesticide use in other countries, Costa Rica continued to use five to ten times the per capita volume of pesticides in comparison to a selection of other Latin American countries from 1982 to 1984 (WHO 1989: 28). Although bananas accounted for an estimated 35 percent of the pesticides used in that country, the expansion of the nontraditional sector added significantly to the high level of pesticide consumption (Trivelato and Wesseling 1991: 2).

More generally, as the economic crisis and the collapse of the cotton sector curbed pesticide imports and use in the region during the early

Table 4-3 Pesticide Imports into Nicaragua,
1980–1990

Year	Kilograms/liters	Cost (millions of US$)
1980	9,929,999	25.0
1981	10,312,000	37.0
1982	5,543,000	20.0
1983	9,987,000	42.0
1984	9,398,000	38.0
1985	9,491,000	55.0
1986	12,165,000	64.0
1987	9,871,000	58.0
1988	7,142,791	47.9
1989	4,522,106	35.6
1990	1,921,634	13.6

SOURCE: Appel et al. 1991.

1980s, other sectors generated increasing demand and kept pesticide imports relatively high throughout the rest of the 1980s (Figure 4-1). The small but growing nontraditional export sector became a dynamic contributor to the regional pesticide market. The increase in pesticide sales in this sector was premised in part upon the increasing number of new pesticide users. As small farmers were transformed from subsistence or local-market producers into export crop farmers, their reliance on the agrochemical technology increased.

These new export farmers often depended on their more traditional sources of information for pest control, which included the advice of government technicians, when they were available, or more frequently the local pesticide distributor (Contreras 1990; Campos 1986). In some instances exporters, through contracts with small producers to purchase their harvested crops, would provide technical packages, which included specific chemicals and application schedules as well as field visits by company technicians. This practice became increasingly common in the latter part of the 1980s. In other cases, exporters provided pesticide application teams, which visited producer plots on a calendar schedule to apply pesticides, a service for which the producers were charged at the time of payment for their harvest (Murray et al. 1989).

Shifting crop patterns began to transform pesticide use throughout the Caribbean Basin. For example, one of the early entries into export vegetable production was Guatemala. A study of changing pesticide use patterns in the municipality of Almolonga (department of Quezalte-

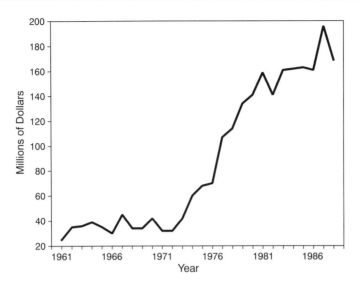

Figure 4-1   Central American Pesticide Imports. SOURCE: U.S. Department of Agriculture, World Agricultural Trade Index.

nango), where vegetable production (primarily for domestic and Central American markets) now dominates local agriculture, found that although only 1 percent of the farmers used pesticides in 1960, by 1975 90 percent were using the technology (Campos 1986). With the rise of nontraditional export agriculture throughout Central America and the Caribbean in the 1980s, this pattern was repeated.

Ecological Disruption and the Return to the Pesticide Treadmill

Predictably, with the re-creation of the chemical-intensive agricultural export model, some of the same problems found in the previous era reemerged in the new development efforts. The most notable was the increasing disruption of the agroecosystem, but somewhat surprisingly, the ecological disruption appears to have re-created ecologically based crisis conditions faster than during the cotton era. Cotton went through a cyclical process of rising and falling production that, after thirty years or more, finally fell into an irreversible decline. The new nontraditional sector in some instances entered a crisis phase after less than a decade of development. While it is still too early to conclude that a full-blown crisis is inevitably forthcoming, several cases of nontraditional agricultural development in Central America and the Caribbean illustrate at least the tendency toward a reoccurrence of crises in the current development efforts.

Signs of a buildup of ecological disruption associated with pesticide use can be found in many countries and nontraditional crops. Guatemala was an early leader in the nontraditional export sector. A USAID-funded survey of such producers in the Guatemalan highlands in 1987 found that 82 percent of those interviewed reported increasing pesticide use, a general but useful indicator of the likely re-creation of the treadmill effect described in Chapter 3 (CICP 1988:48). When asked if pests were becoming "stronger" each season, 85 percent answered yes. Farmers also identified several particular pesticides, including methamidophos, methyl parathion, aldrin, methomyl, and propineb, as increasingly ineffective at controlling pests. All of these chemicals are among the most toxic and most widely used insecticides available in Central America.

Similar evidence was generated by a regional survey that found a pattern of increasing pesticide use throughout the region (Conroy et al. forthcoming), with farmers from Guatemala and Costa Rica, the countries with the most developed nontraditional agricultural sectors, reporting an almost universal increase in pesticide use over three years earlier (Table 4-4). The increase took the form of not only extra applications but also stronger doses per application, as demonstrated by the following anecdotal observation: "Symptomatic of the increasing problems of pest control and pesticide use is the common-thread finding that farmers are continually having to use greater quantities of pesticides to do the job. For example, some farmers no longer use Bayer caps (25cc) as units of measure for pesticide mixtures, instead they use pounds, cups or eights-of-a-liter as units of measure" (CICP 1988:52). The combination of indicators suggests that the dynamic of the pesticide treadmill, which developed in cotton, was also well under way in the new nontraditional sector. Increased pest resistance was accompa-

Table 4-4 Reported Increase in Pesticide Use

Question: *Did you spray more or less often three years ago?*

	More often	Less often	Same	Total
Guatemala	1 (2.22%)	40 (88.89%)	4 (8.89%)	45
El Salvador	14 (21.88%)	36 (56.25%)	14 (21.88%)	64
Honduras	12 (27.91%)	24 (55.81%)	7 (16.28%)	43
Costa Rica	0 (0)	21 (91.30%)	2 (8.70%)	23

SOURCE: Conroy et al. forthcoming.

nied by increased pesticide use, which was in turn leading to less effective chemicals, greater pest problems, and still further increased pesticide use.

Another recent survey (Universidad del Valle 1993) suggests that ecological disruption may be leading to further problems. Soil quality and soil erosion may be the most powerful indicators of the ecological well-being of nontraditional agriculture. Survey results suggest that nontraditional crops have seriously undermined the long-term ecological sustainability of agriculture in the highlands through the degradation of soil.

One indicator of soil quality is the amount of leaf litter or mulch on the ground surface. This material is an important control of erosion and holds humidity in the soil. It also provides habitat for natural enemies to pests and contributes to the organic content of the soil so necessary for plant growth. The quantity of leaf litter in traditional crops (corn and beans) was found to be much greater than in nontraditionals. The quantity of earthworms in a plot of soil is also an indicator of soil quality, as well as an indicator of pesticide damage. The survey found far fewer earthworms in broccoli plots than in corn plots, and no earthworms among the heaviest user of pesticides, snow peas.

Erosion is an even more important indicator of the ecological effect of nontraditionals. The rate of erosion in broccoli plots in San José Pinula, Guatemala, was twice the rate found in traditional corn plots in the same community. Finally, the level of aluminum residues in soil, an indicator of possible toxic buildup of microelements from fertilization, was also measured. Aluminum residues were significantly higher for broccoli (although still not at phytotoxic levels) than for corn, suggesting potential future problems with declining soil productivity due to toxic buildup.

Increasing pesticide use almost invariably translates into increasing input costs, which are exacerbated by the tendency for pesticide prices to increase as well. In the Guatemalan highlands pesticide purchase, application, and related technical assistance costs accounted for 22.5 percent of total production costs for nontraditional crops like snow peas, broccoli, cauliflower, and lettuce (CICP 1988 : 55). Relying on government data on credit requirements for various crops, investigators found that melon production required up to $2,206 in credits per hectare for pesticide-related costs, and snow peas required even more. Another study of pesticide costs in Guatemala (exclusive of other pesticide-related production costs) found that one nontraditional, snow peas, required higher pesticide expenditures per manzana (0.705 hectare) than either cotton or bananas, the two crops that historically consumed the greatest volume and variety of pesticides in the region (Campos 1986) (Figure 4-2).

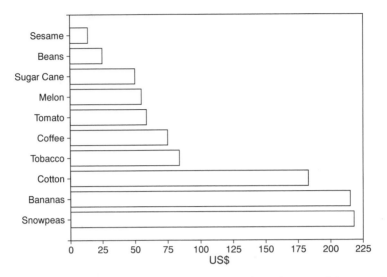

Figure 4-2   Cost of Pesticide Application in Selected Areas of Guatemala, 1986 (US$/Manzana). SOURCE: Campos 1986.

In less than a decade from the initial promotional efforts in nontraditional export agriculture, pesticide use and ecological disruption were increasing in a pattern reminiscent of the previous era of development. Early indicators suggest the pesticide treadmill was accelerating, with rising pest problems and pesticide costs squeezing increasingly pesticide-dependent producers. But the early indicators went beyond the dynamic of those economic costs to include renewed human health problems in the agroexport sector.

Health Effects of Pesticides in Nontraditional Agriculture

As pesticide use rose in nontraditional agriculture, so did pesticide-related illness rates. The access of small farmers to highly toxic chemicals was a primary factor in the increasing number of poisonings, but the problem was also driven by the kinds of chemicals required for nontraditional agricultural production. Farmers relied on some of the most toxic chemicals available in the international market, particularly organophosphate and carbamate insecticides, to control the proliferating numbers and types of pests. For example, 23 percent (ten out of forty-four) of the most commonly used pesticides in Guatemalan nontraditional agriculture were classified as extremely or highly toxic by the WHO, chemicals to which only trained and licensed applicators have access in the United States (Hoppin 1991: 179–183). In addition, a large quantity of pesticides that were banned or never registered in their country of manufacture continue to be exported to Central America (Foundation for Advancements in Science and Education 1993; Marquardt and Glassman 1990).

The high-toxicity insecticides were required in part because most of the less toxic organochlorines had been discontinued in reaction to their capacity to remain as residues on produce for relatively long periods after their application, as well as their decreasing effectiveness in controlling resistant pests and their capacity to produce secondary pest problems. The far more toxic, but much more rapidly degrading organophosphates and carbamates were the primary types of insecticides that continued to be allowed for use on these crops by the EPA. Chemicals with EPA registration for use on specific crops normally had tolerance levels for residues on those crops, also set by EPA, which if not exceeded would allow shipments of these crops to pass Food and Drug Administration monitoring upon entry into the United States.

As cotton production declined in the 1980s, overall pesticide illness rates declined as well. For example, the frequency of pesticide poisoning in León, Nicaragua, declined in the last two years of the 1980s along with cotton production (Keifer and Pacheco 1991). Yet while illness rates for the entire country declined because of the decline in the volume of pesticides used and the decline in the number of people exposed to pesticides in the cotton sector, pesticide poisoning remained quite high among smaller populations in the nontraditional agriculture sector. In Guatemala, a study of nontraditional producers found that 29 percent (42 out of 145) had been poisoned at least once (CICP 1988:50). Another study of two nontraditional agricultural communities in Guatemala found a much higher frequency of pesticide poisoning, with 68 percent of the farmers reporting at least one lifetime episode of acute pesticide poisoning (USCG 1990). A third study found that 50 percent of Guatemalan nontraditional producers had been poisoned at least once (Hoppin 1989).

One regional survey attempted to provide more precise data. Small-scale melon producers were surveyed in four countries and were asked if they had experienced one or more poisoning episodes in the previous two years (Conroy et al. forthcoming). As Table 4-5 demonstrates, reported illness rates were high in all four countries, with Guatemala and Costa Rica rates at over 50 percent.

When these rates are compared with data from León, Nicaragua (long considered the worst example of pesticide use and poisoning), they show how serious the problem is in nontraditional agriculture. Keifer and Pacheco (1991) estimated that 13.5 percent of the farmers and farm workers in León were poisoned in 1989 (from all sectors, not just non-

Table 4-5 Nontraditional Export Farmers Reporting Poisonings in the
Last Two Years

| | Number of farmers (percent of total) | | |
	Poisoned	Not poisoned	Total
Guatemala	26 (57.78)	19 (42.22)	45
El Salvador	21 (28.38)	53 (71.62)	74
Honduras	13 (28.89)	32 (71.11)	45
Costa Rica	14 (56.00)	11 (44.00)	25

SOURCE: Conroy et al. forthcoming.

traditionals).[8] If we double the single-year rate from León to make it roughly equivalent to the two-year regional rates reported by Conroy et al., we can see that the León rate is about the same as that reported in the Honduran and Salvadoran nontraditional sector. However, the Costa Rican and Guatemalan illness rates are far worse than that of the notorious department of León. The relatively lower Nicaraguan rate is probably due in part to the predominant role that corn, which uses considerably less pesticide than either nontraditionals or cotton, has played in the past several years in León's agriculture. The comparison of reported illness rates, while crude, nevertheless is suggestive of the seriousness of the problem related to pesticide poisoning in the region's nontraditional export agriculture sector.

Acute illness is not the only cause for alarm. Some of the most heavily used pesticides in nontraditional agriculture have recently been associated with long-term and permanent health problems. Sixteen pesticides identified in one study of Guatemalan nontraditional agriculture were associated with cancer, birth defects, organ malfunctions, and other chronic disorders (Hoppin 1991:179–183). One of them, the organophosphate methamidophos, gives ample indication of the kinds of long-term hazards that may be developing in this sector. In the Guatemalan highlands, methamidophos was the most frequently reported cause of acute poisoning among nontraditional export farmers interviewed for one study funded by the USAID (CICP 1988:50). Similarly, the three most commonly reported sources of pesticide poisoning in the more recent regional survey were methamidophos and the carbamates methomyl and carbofuran (Conroy et al. forthcoming) (Table 4-6). These three pesticides accounted for 83.5 percent of the instances in which farmers could name the chemical that had caused an incident identifiable as a pesticide-related illness.

In a recently reported study (Rosenstock et al. 1991) of permanent

Table 4-6 Most Frequently Reported Sources of Pesticide-Related Illness

Country	n	Metho-myl	%	Meth-amido-phos	%	Carbo-furan	%
El Salvador	45	13	37.1%	13	37.1%	1	2.9%
Honduras	42	10	23.8%	12	28.6%	18	42.95
Costa Rica	26	13	50.0%	6	23.1%	0	0%

SOURCE: Conroy et al. forthcoming.

neurological effects caused by organophosphate poisoning, researchers found an array of reduced neurological functions among a group of thirty-six Nicaraguan farm laborers who had experienced an acute episode of pesticide poisoning at some point in the previous two years. Poisoned workers were given a battery of neuropsychological tests developed by the WHO, as were a control group of people never poisoned. The workers who had been poisoned showed statistically significant reductions in normal neurological functions on five out of six of the WHO tests and had similarly poorer scores on three out of six additional tests. The reduced neurological functions included verbal and visual attention, visual memory, visuomotor speed, sequencing and problem solving, and motor steadiness and dexterity.

A second study (McConnell et al. 1993) by the same research team found that poisoned workers were also experiencing peripheral nervous system damage, such as permanent reduction of feeling and strength in the hands, arms, and most frequently in the legs and feet, which was independent of the previously discovered effects of organophosphates on the brain. Particularly disturbing was the fact that methamidophos, a leading source of acute poisoning among nontraditional producers, was the primary pesticide associated with permanent neurological problems. These findings of neurological effects suggest that acute pesticide poisonings may be contributing to long-term reduction in the quality of life and the lifetime productivity of poisoning victims. The high rate of pesticide poisonings among nontraditional producers suggests that pesticides may be an even greater problem for the rural populace than has been generally recognized to date.

Conclusion

The return to chemical-intensive export agriculture appears to have generated a return of many of the ecological and public health problems that accompanied the previous development process. Pest resistance and pesticide use appear to be escalating even faster than in the cotton era. Although fewer people, less hectarage, and smaller volumes of pesticides are involved in the much-smaller-scale, nontraditional export venture, it appears that among the populations involved, the problems may be of comparable severity. More important, contrary to the assurances of USAID and chemical-industry representatives, the problems are growing along with the expansion of the nontraditional sector.

In fact, the notion that the crisis of the Lost Decade could be resolved by a return to a development strategy similar to the one that preceded the crisis reflects an incredibly shortsighted vision of the needs of the Third World. In this context, there should be little wonder that pesticide problems were not addressed in a more serious manner. Why should they be taken seriously when the whole range of development problems of which they were a part were given such desultory and superficial attention?

Clearly, pesticide technology has shown the capacity to re-create the problems associated with the cotton era, but it appears that the new nontraditional export crops also represent a much more complex and diverse development sector than cotton, and consequently the problems and changes occurring within that sector are also more complex. In particular, there appears to be an array of socioeconomic effects that both are reminiscent of the cotton era and suggest a considerable variation from the dynamics seen in the cotton boom. The greater complexity of the development process based on nontraditional exports warrants a more detailed look at several case studies of current development projects. In so doing, the next chapter will try to determine if the tendency of pesticides to generate crises in the agroexport sector holds up across different crops and different social, economic, and political settings.

5

Pesticides and Social Inequity in Nontraditional Agriculture

One of the most striking effects of the cotton era, and of the Golden Age of Central American development more generally, was the widening disparity between rich and poor that occurred amid unprecedented growth. Increasing landlessness, unemployment, and underemployment eroded the already impoverished condition of the rural majority during the 1970s. It was the desperate plight of the displaced and impoverished peasantry, alongside the growing concentration of wealth in the agrarian sector, that ignited social discontent and rebellion in various parts of Central America.

The social and political dimensions of the regional crisis were not lost on the development planners promoting the new development strategy of nontraditional agriculture. The new vision for Central American and Caribbean development defined by the Kissinger Commission Report, the Caribbean Basin Initiative, and related policy statements included explicit proposals to overcome the social inequity and consequent political instability of the previous era. The promotion of nontraditional agriculture was a central component of this vision. One recent report funded by USAID described the contribution to improved social equity expected from the nontraditional crops: "They are perceived to hold great promise because:—first they tend to be labor intensive thus helping to address the region's unemployment problems;—second, they can often be grown on comparatively small parcels of land, thus achieving 'higher' use of the land and bringing development opportunities within the range of small land holders and providing a wider distribution of benefits among the population;—and third, they tend to be high valued, thus helping improve the flow of hard currency into the region" (Alberti 1991:i). Nontraditional agriculture was seen as more than a means to stimulate growth (and improve economic prospects for debt servicing). By improving economic opportunities for small farmers and rural laborers, the strategy sought to overcome some of the glaring inequity and diffuse the social and political discontent that plagued the previous development era.

In search of the promised economic opportunity, tens of thousands of small farmers entered nontraditional agriculture during the 1980s, frequently contracting with larger transnational companies which processed and exported the new crops (Glover and Kusterer 1990). Many thousands more farm laborers found employment on the large-scale and, again, often transnational corporate farms, as the strategy began to transform the traditional social and economic structure of the agrarian sector in several countries.

But preliminary evidence suggests that the new development strategy has generated decidedly different results from those promised by planners. Paradoxically, the failure to address the pesticide-related problems associated with the previous cotton era appears to be contributing to a regeneration of some of the same social and economic conditions that were the foundation of the previous crisis—the same conditions the current development strategy was promulgated to address.

To understand the somewhat complex socioeconomic dynamics that have accompanied the pesticide-related ecological disruption occurring in the new development process, it will be useful to explore several nontraditional development projects in some detail, first in the Dominican Republic and then in Honduras and Guatemala. Drawing upon those cases, this chapter will then return to the regional level to explore some provocative implications for the perpetuation of crisis tendencies and social inequity emerging from the nontraditional strategy.

The Dominican Republic as a CBI Showcase

The Dominican Republic's status as the showcase of Caribbean Basin development in the early 1980s was premised upon that country's success in both nontraditional agricultural and industrial production (Mathieson 1988) (Table 4-1). Dominican nontraditional agriculture was particularly successful, leading the region in attracting foreign investment, with one writer for *The Economist* projecting that during 1986–1991, the Dominican Republic would be: "the Caribbean country which offers by far the most important agricultural and agro-industry (investment) opportunities" (Raynolds 1991 : 19).

Dominican agricultural exports included a wide range of crops largely unknown outside particular ethnic groups. Most notable were the oriental vegetables, such as Japanese eggplant, fuzzy squash, bitter melon, and long beans, which were produced for a primarily Asian population in the United States, Canada, and elsewhere. Although these specialty crops were little known, they nevertheless came to occupy an important place among Dominican exports. The most reliable estimate placed oriental vegetables at roughly 11 percent of earnings from nontraditional agricultural exports in 1987 (Raynolds 1992), although Santo Domingo's leading newspaper estimated that these crops accounted for as much as 25 percent of such earnings (Raynolds 1991).

Satellite, or outgrower, farming systems were predominant in the production of oriental vegetables and many other nontraditional crops. Oriental vegetables were grown by two thousand to three thousand very small-scale producers, who sold their produce to a dozen or more local exporters (Raynolds 1991). In some instances producers worked under contract with the exporters, who in turn provided credits, inputs such as seeds and pesticides, and technical assistance. But among growers of oriental vegetables, it was more common for producers to farm under much less structured arrangements. During harvest periods it was not unusual to find producers driving from one local packing shed to another, with their day's harvest of long beans draped over a motorcycle seat, as they negotiated with buyers for the best price (Murray et al. 1989). Buyers and exporters, in these cases, had little knowledge of or control over producer cultivation practices.

This form of satellite farming appealed to risk-averse exporters. By making little or no preharvest investment, exporters could pass on losses from adverse market conditions, overproduction, decreased demand, and other risks to the producer. Farmers also bore most of the financial risk of the common agricultural problems associated with weather, pests, and transportation. Exporters maintained low capital risk, often investing only in low-cost, concrete-block packing sheds with refrigeration units and various sorting and packing tables, located near the farming communities.

Oriental vegetable farmers relied on a wide range of chemicals for pest control. They frequently applied "cocktails," a mixture of several chemicals purchased from local pesticide merchants. These pesticides were applied on a calendar schedule to control existing or anticipated pest problems. In the now familiar pattern of pesticide use and abuse, farmers used chemicals relatively indiscriminately, with little appreciation of the ecological damage of their farming practices. But the predictable manifestation of ecological problems was not long in appearing.

Initially, pesticide problems did not appear in the form of increasing crop losses or pest problems, as had been the case in cotton. Instead, they emerged as economic losses due to regulatory actions once the Dominican produce reached its destination in the United States. In 1987 and 1988, the Dominican Republic held the dubious distinction of having the highest rate of illegal pesticide residues in samples of produce imported into the United States and has been among the leaders ever since.[1] Of the samples taken by the U.S. Food and Drug Administration (FDA), 12.2 percent (217 out of 1,697) were in violation of government standards for allowable residues in food (Tables 5-1 and 5-2).

The oriental vegetable sector was a significant contributor to the residue problem. The uncontrolled use of pesticides by satellite producers was generating major problems in the nontraditional export sector. By 1988, individual exporters were reporting losses due to residue on ship-

Table 5-1 Rejections of Nontraditional Produce Shipments
by FDA for Pesticide Residues

	Fiscal year[a]						
	1985	1986	1987	1988	1989	1990	1991
Dominican Republic							
Total samples	103	165	481	1216	2531	701	427
Pesticide violations	5	9	45	172	1354	252	138
Percent of total	4.8	5.4	9.3	14.1	53.5	35.9	32.3
Other violations[b]	126 over 7 years						
Guatemala							
Total samples	35	99	181	272	249	439	258
Pesticide violations	10	0	3	18	55	120	18
Percent of total	28.6	0	1.6	6.6	22.1	27.3	6.6
Other violations	52 over 7 years						

SOURCE: FDA, National Import Detention System.

[a]The fiscal year runs from October 1 to September 30. Fiscal year 1991 includes data only through June, but imports from Latin America are normally low during the last quarter of the fiscal year and should not change the detention rates significantly.
[b]Includes insect and other filth, spoilage, unregistered additives and dyes, heavy metals, and others.

Table 5-2 FDA Detentions FY 1989[a],
Selected Countries

Country	Number of detentions	Country	Number of detentions
Mexico	1,919	Barbados	5
Dominican Republic	1,429	Grenada	5
Belize	3	Aruba	24
Bahamas	25	Guatemala	87
Turks and Caicos Islands	6	Honduras	50
Cayman Isles	3	El Salvador	160
Antigua	3	Nicaragua	1
Haiti	38	Costa Rica	85
U.S. Virgin Islands	1	Panama	37
British Virgin Islands	6	Jamaica	39
Dominica	1	United States	
Martinique	1	(U.S. goods returned)	195
St. Vincent	1	Global detentions	26,013

SOURCE: FDA 1989.

[a]Inconsistencies between FDA reports cited in this chapter are attributed "to the nature and complexities" of the different data gathering systems, according to the FDA (FDA 1989:1).

ments in the hundreds of thousands of dollars in a single month, with their combined losses reaching an estimated $2.5 million in the 1989 season (Murray et al. 1989:1).

The appeal of the low-investment, low-risk satellite farming system was fading fast as the FDA imposed cropwide automatic detentions[2] on five oriental vegetables in 1988, requiring that every Dominican shipment be sampled prior to acceptance into the United States. Before the automatic detention, many exporters had found the threat of relatively infrequent rejections preferable to the additional investment necessary for controlling crop production and pesticide use. For example, one exporter chose to use several brand names on subsequent shipments after one of his shipments was rejected, feeling certain that most of his produce would get past the infrequent FDA sampling (Murray et al. 1989). Those exporters were accustomed to an FDA sampling rate of 3.4 percent (Mott and Snyder 1988). When the FDA began inspecting 100 percent of shipments, the exporters faced far greater losses from rejections, on top of the extra costs for laboratory testing generated by FDA policy.

As if the residue problems were not enough, producers of oriental vegetables soon found themselves on the pesticide treadmill, applying an increasing volume and variety of chemicals to control increasing pest problems. By 1988, producers in La Vega, the primary oriental vegetable farming zone, found one small insect, *Thrips palmi*, completely out of control. Farmers reported applying as many as nine different recommended insecticides during the 1989 season with little or no effect. Some farmers reported losing up to 100 percent of their crop. One producer complained that a small spider had previously kept the thrips in check, but the spider was no longer to be found in the oriental vegetable fields, presumably a victim of the broad-spectrum effects of pesticides. The producers soon found that the risks of excessive residues on their crops meant very little, as they poured ever more chemicals onto the crops merely to salvage some portion of their harvest.

Then the final blow came on May 8, 1989, when the USDA placed an emergency quarantine on all imports of five oriental vegetables, not because they contained illegal residues (the jurisdiction for which in any case was the FDA's, not the USDA's) but because USDA inspectors found the Dominican produce to be infested with thrips when it was checked at the port of entry into the United States. The quarantine, intended to protect U.S. agriculture from the introduction of foreign pests, when combined with the FDA's automatic detentions and the preharvest losses to pesticide-resistant pests, left oriental vegetable producers with declining yields and no market.

Some exporters shipped what produce they could harvest to Canada, where they found less stringent controls on residues and pests. But the loss of the primary U.S. market was more than the sector could overcome. By the 1989–1990 season, the seven largest exporters of oriental vegetables reported a 57 percent decrease in the area under cultivation (Murray 1989a). With packing and processing operations idle, government and industry sources projected a loss of $16 million to $35 million for the year, and oriental vegetable shipments to the United States almost disappeared from the export profile of the Dominican Republic (Figure 5-1).[3]

Although the pesticide-driven problems in oriental vegetables were a major concern, they represented only one part of an ecologically based economic and social crisis that was emerging by the late 1980s in the Dominican Republic. Several years earlier, a U.S. entomologist had warned of an impending disaster in Constanza Valley. Once a primary vegetable-producing zone on the island, Constanza's agricultural production had been undermined by excessive pesticide use by the mid-1980s. As the visiting entomologist reported, pesticides had generated an explosive outbreak of a highly resistant secondary pest, the greenhouse whitefly (*Trialeurodes vaporariorum*), and had so devastated the agroecosystem that "the valley is unfortunately void of a natural enemy complex to attack the greenhouse whitefly," making the development of alternative IPM strategies far more difficult (Murray et al. 1989: Appendix). Consequently, most agricultural projects had been located in other parts of the country. But the nontraditional producers in the surrounding communities paid little heed to the warnings from Constanza and soon were deeply immersed in their own ecological nightmare.

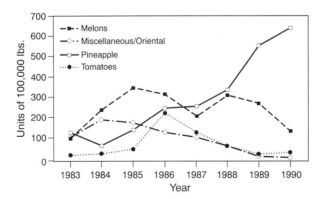

Figure 5-1 Nontraditional Produce Shipments to the United States from the Dominican Republic. SOURCE: Annual summary of fresh fruit and vegetable shipments, USDA Market Research Service.

The Dominican tomato and melon producers of the Azua Valley battled increasing pest resistance and secondary pests during the latter half of the 1980s. At first technicians for one large-scale processing and exporting company blamed the company's small contractors, asserting that the farmers used primitive production practices that created both pest problems and marginal productivity (Murray 1989a). For example, technicians reported that producers often did not use the pesticides the company provided (the cost of which was subtracted from the farmer's payment at the time of harvest), preferring to sell them and substitute less expensive alternatives. To cope with the small farmers' resistance to high technology and high-cost production schemes, the company decided to take greater control of farmer pest-control practices through the addition of a company-prepared technological package to the provisions required under the farmers' preplanting contract. Under the new technological package, the company sent its own crews to each farmer's plot to apply pesticides on a calendar schedule. Farmers could not avoid using the chemicals or paying for them.

In late 1988, the third year of the new package, the Azua Valley experienced an explosive outbreak of the cotton whitefly (*Bemisia tabaci*). Like the greenhouse whitefly in Constanza, the cotton whitefly was a secondary pest, the product of heavy pesticide use that eliminated the pest's natural enemies and allowed uncontrolled growth of the whitefly population. The outbreak resulted in a 58.7 percent reduction of fresh tomato exports and an overall loss of $5.9 million (domestic and export, processed and fresh) (Murray 1989a:2). The area planted in tomatoes declined by 48 percent in 1989, and yields per hectare decreased by 20 to 25 percent.

Now the producers, unlike company technicians, placed the blame for the pest problems on the technological package mandated by the company contracts. The spokesperson for an association of more than five thousand small farmers attributed the whitefly outbreak to the frequent pesticide applications by company technicians. He complained that small producers traditionally were reluctant to use pesticides because they did not consider the increased yields sufficient to offset the increased costs. He went on to observe that although the whitefly had been troublesome in the past, small farmers had never faced such severe losses until they were required to use the intensive spraying program.

The whitefly similarly devastated the Azua Valley's melon sector at the same time. Small farmers reported that the whitefly was also moving from the cash crops into such basic subsistence crops as beans, not only restricting income options for small producers but also undermining the traditional peasant safety net of subsistence agriculture. The squeeze on small producers was tightened when the Secretaría del Estado de Agricultura took the drastic step of imposing a moratorium on the planting of all but a few crops in the region, such as corn and sorghum, in order to reduce the host crops on which the whitefly could survive during the off-season for melons and tomatoes (Murray and Hoppin 1992).

It appears that not only the economic growth that development planners had hoped for but also the promised improvement in economic opportunities for small producers and the rural poor were erased by the pesticide crisis. Two thousand to three thousand small-scale growers of oriental vegetables were plunged into severe economic hardship as their primary source of income disappeared, leaving them with heavy debts incurred to pursue the promises of nontraditional agriculture. Similarly, several thousand farm workers in the Azua Valley, mostly women and children, lost their primary source of annual income with the decline of the tomato and melon harvests. The estimated loss of two million pesos ($300,000) in local wages due to the whitefly implied further hardship for these laborers and their families.

The ecological disruption caused by pesticides in Dominican nontraditional agriculture led to major pest problems across a range of crops. The social and economic disruption was nothing short of a crisis for the nontraditional sector. The impressive growth anticipated by Dominican industry sources was never realized. Instead, the Dominican Republic fell into an accelerated, albeit more localized, version of the ecological-cum-economic crisis seen in the earlier cotton era of Central America. It appears that this crisis has re-created some of the social factors, such as the increasing impoverishment of small farmers and the rural labor force, that characterized the growing inequity between rich and poor of the previous era.

But a further look at the effect of pesticides in the new development strategy reveals that the nontraditional development process is still more complex than the Dominican case has suggested. Honduras provides a second case study to determine if the Dominican crisis reflects a pattern inherent in the development process, or merely an isolated aberration.

The Honduran Melon Export Boom

The most successful project in Honduras's efforts to stimulate nontraditional agricultural exports grew out of the collapse of the country's previous venture into cotton production. The Honduran cotton industry never compared with the grand scale seen in neighboring Guatemala, El Salvador, and Nicaragua. At its peak in 1978, Honduras cultivated little more than eighteen thousand hectares of cotton (Table 2–1). But the lesser scale of the Honduran cotton sector did not reduce the economic disruption of the regionwide cotton crisis within the Honduran cotton zones. As cotton production fell during the 1980s, serious social and economic problems developed. The Honduran Secretaría de Recursos Naturales estimated that the number of families benefiting from cotton-related activities fell from 85,741 in the 1975–1980 period to 57,617 during the 1981–1986 period (Bueso 1987).

Cotton farming continued to decline until it virtually disappeared from the department of Choluteca, historically the primary cotton-producing area. A representative of the cotton producers' organization, Cooperativa Agropecüaria Algodonera del Sur, projected that only fifty hectares would be planted in Choluteca for the 1991 season (Murray 1991). The collapse of the cotton sector in this department was particularly disastrous. Hundreds of cotton farmers went out of business during a period when livestock and sugar production, other mainstays of the local economy, also declined, leading to an estimated unemployment rate among the male workforce of over 60 percent and a severe outward migration from and depopulation of the department (Stonich 1993).

USAID and other international development agencies began promoting new nontraditional crops in the early 1980s in an effort to help overcome the economic crisis and reactivate the local economy. Melons (primarily cantaloupe, to a lesser extent honeydew, and more recently watermelon) were among several crops that USAID considered appropriate for promotion because they could generate considerable economic growth locally and could involve large numbers of small producers "to a significant extent" (USAID 1990:16).

In 1983 USAID encouraged a group of producers to split off from the main melon enterprise in the area, United Brands' Productos Acuáticos y Terrestres, S.A. (Patsa), and form a small- and medium-scale cooperative, Cooperativa Regional de Horticultores Sureños Limitada (Crehsul). It grew to be the largest melon cooperative in the department, with fifty producers farming two to ten hectares each by 1989 (Murray 1991). Small producers accounted for as much as half the land under melon cultivation by the end of the decade (USAID 1990).

Melons were produced either through contract arrangements, such as existed within Crehsul or with Patsa, or under a more conventional plantation system employed by several transnationals and large-scale Honduran companies, which entered the melon sector in the latter part of the 1980s. In both cases, it appears that pesticides were heavily and excessively used to assure crop yields and to meet the various quality standards required of produce imported into the United States.

Pesticides were applied to the melon fields on a calendar schedule, similar to the pattern of the preceding cotton era. Some questioned the continued reliance on the calendar spraying approach. The chief research entomologist for United Brands during the 1970s, Dr. Eugene Ostmark, recalled the initial years of Patsa's melon production: "Patsa had a brilliant field manager. But he really pushed calendar spraying to control aphids, which transmitted a virus to melon plants. We knew by then that it would cause problems, and science has since shown that virus can't be controlled with insecticides. But he didn't believe it. He would say 'see, we don't have any virus.' But the problem was building" (Murray 1991).

Even with a high level of technical assistance, Patsa plunged ahead with a pesticide-based production strategy that promised serious problems for the long-term viability of melon farming. Most melon producers had access to far less skilled technicians than did the transnationals (Byrnes 1989). As the melon sector grew in the late 1980s, the bulk of the day-to-day field decisions about pest control fell on local technicians who had been trained primarily in traditional crops such as cotton, corn, and sugarcane. These technicians had a tendency to rely excessively on pesticides, often recommending applications as a prophylactic measure out of fear of potential pest damage to fields for which they were responsible. Farmers shared this risk aversion and placed further pressure on technicians to use pesticides or made their own independent decisions to apply the chemicals. The tendency toward excessive pesticide use was heightened by local pesticide distributors who, predictably, recommended additional products or increased dosages of pesticides with the appearance of each new pest (Contreras 1990).

As the Patsa entomologist and others had anticipated, pesticide-driven problems were developing in Choluteca's melon sector. During the 1988–1989 season, various pests accounted for an estimated 10 percent reduction in the anticipated harvest. Although the losses were considered significant, they were overshadowed by what was the largest melon harvest to date (Figure 5-2).

Early in the following season the pest problems took a turn for the worse as aphid-borne plant viruses and explosive outbreaks of whiteflies and leaf miners reached crisis proportions, reducing the projected harvest by 45 to 56 percent, with some farmers losing their entire crop. The problem was so severe that one international pest specialist described the situation as "a crisis approaching disaster," raising the question "of whether Choluteca will still be producing melons in 4 to 5 years" (Murray 1991).

Technicians and large producers placed the blame for the crisis on the small-scale producers, some of whom, for lack of resources or knowledge, failed to plow under the melon plants after the harvest. The remaining plants provided a host in which melon pests could survive and

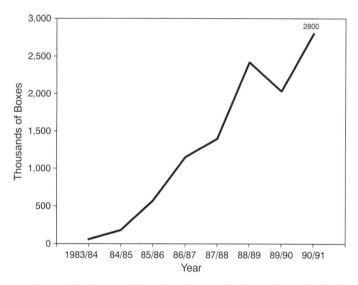

Figure 5-2 Melon Exports from Honduras. A wooden box of cantaloupes contains 9 to 30 melons, depending on grade (size), and weighs 35 to 40 pounds. Melons are planted and harvested in several cycles during a single season, which overlaps two calendar years. The season runs roughly from October to April. SOURCE: 1983/84–1984/85 Byrnes 1989; 1985/86–1989/90 FPX 1990. 1990/91 Preliminary estimate (personal communication, George Garcelon June 28, 1991.

grow during periods when melons were not normally cultivated. Some also pointed to the overall increase in the area planted in melons as creating a reservoir and attraction for pest problems.

But other national and international pest specialists readily admitted that a large part of the problem was linked to the history of frequent pesticide applications, which fostered resistant and secondary pests. One investigation into the problem found that beneficial insects, which normally kept pest populations in check, had virtually disappeared from Choluteca by the end of the 1980s (Marenco 1990). A survey of the whitefly population in the Cholutecan melon fields found less than 1 percent of the whitefly eggs had been parasitized, in contrast to surveys taken in other regions of Honduras, including San Pedro Sula (20 percent parasitized) and Zamorano (15 percent parasitized).[4] These same researchers also found a 200 percent increase in leaf miner eggs in the melon fields, another indicator of the disappearance of the natural controls provided by beneficials.

Pesticide application rates had increased with the buildup of pest problems. The pest control schedule provided by Crehsul to its produc-

Table 5-3 Pesticide Application Schedule,
First Melon Cycle, 1989–1990

Days after plant sprouts	Insecticide applied	Fungicide applied
4	Methamidophos	Benlate
10	Perfekthion	Benlate
16	Methamidophos	Ridomil
22	*Bacillus thuringiensis*	—
28	*Bacillus thuringiensis*	Dithane
34	*Bacillus thuringiensis* Methamidophos	Ridomil
40	*Bacillus thuringiensis*	—
44	—	Daconil Benlate
46	Ambush	Daconil
52	Methomyl	Daconil
58	Ambush	—

SOURCE: Crehsul.

ers for the 1989–1990 season called for eleven applications during the short crop cycle of two and one half months (Table 5-3).[5] Nearly half of these applications involved highly toxic insecticides. A producer survey reported even higher application rates of nineteen per season (Marenco 1990), with some reportedly applying pesticides every two days. By 1990, pesticide use in melons was rapidly approaching the rates historically found in Central American cotton production.

Choluteca's pesticide-driven crisis hit particularly hard among the small producers in the melon sector. Like the larger producers, many small producers incurred serious economic losses from the failed harvest. The crisis drove many producers, large and small, from the melon sector, but unlike the large producers, the small operators found their economic losses compounded by policy changes among some of the transnational exporters who bought their harvests.

Patsa, which had been the largest contractor of small and medium producers, shifted a significant portion of its melon production away from contract farming and into estate, or plantation, farming for the 1990–1991 season, in part because the company felt it could not effectively control pesticide use among its contract producers (Murray 1991). Patsa planted four to five tracts of 125 to 140 hectares each under its own field management, shifting 10 to 20 percent of the Honduran land previously cultivated by smaller producers into estate production. An estimated eighteen to twenty small and medium producers dropped by Patsa moved to Crehsul for the 1990–1991 season.

Along with Patsa's shift away from contracts with small producers, Crehsul also began to change in ways that indicated that small-producer opportunities were dwindling. Crehsul's membership increased as the fall planting began for the 1990–1991 season, as it had in recent years with the expansion of the melon sector, but this time the new members were not new producers who had been drawn into the melon sector, as in the past. Instead, they were small farmers expelled from Patsa or larger producers who had obtained financing for the coming season from outside the existing credit system, mostly from Miami-based brokers.

The changing character of Crehsul and Patsa suggested a significant shift in Choluteca's melon sector. For example, individual farm sizes among small and medium-sized producers in Crehsul showed a marked change, with average farm size nearly doubling from 7.86 manzanas in 1989–1990 to 13.51 manzanas in 1990–1991 (Figure 5-3). This shift toward larger farms was almost entirely the result of better-financed operators' entering the melon sector, and not an indicator of increasing good fortune among the smaller producers.

Data from other operations confirm that the structure of Honduran melon production was changing. The Cooperativa Agropecüaria Algo-

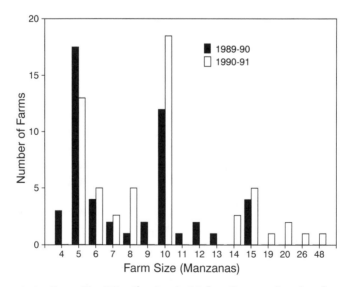

Figure 5-3 Farm Size Distribution in Melon Cooperative, Southern Honduras. SOURCE: Murray 1991.

donera del Sur, which had recently converted from cotton to melons, reported a shift in farm size from an average of 8.5 manzanas in 1989–1990 (11 producers, 94 manzanas) to 11.4 manzanas (35 producers, 400 manzanas) in 1990–1991. If this pattern continued alone, it would indicate a significant reduction in the role of small-scale production in the melon sector. But early reports from the 1990–1991 harvest suggested that these changes were the result of further obstacles to small-producer participation in melon production, obstacles that were also attributable, at least indirectly, to the pesticide-driven crisis.

Small farmers were given new hope of overcoming the previous year's crisis as unusual weather conditions significantly reduced the aphid populations in the melon fields before the fall planting for the 1990–1991 season. A severe drought during the normally rainy summer months meant that the growth of weeds and summer crops that sustained the aphids, plant viruses, and other pests during the off-season was far below normal at the time of the fall melon planting. Subsequent late rains significantly reduced the first harvest in late 1990, but the second and third cycles in early 1991 yielded bumper harvests as ample soil moisture and the absence of aphids boosted melon yields to an all-time high. Preliminary reports placed the total 1990-1991 harvests at 2.8 million boxes, well above previous highs (Figure 5-2).

The reduction in aphid problems was also a product of the increased use of Integrated Pest Management (IPM) techniques, such as the introduction of plant barriers to keep pests out of the melon fields and the elimination of weeds and postharvest melon plants, which served as hosts for the pest populations during the off-season, along with far more selective pesticide use. The IPM techniques were particularly effective among small producers working with a technician trained at the Escuela Panamericana Agricola (Panamerican Agricultural School) in Zamorano, Honduras, although the relative weight of importance of the IPM efforts and technical assistance versus the unusual climatic conditions remains difficult to ascertain. The increase in yields reported by producers across the region, many of whom did not benefit from the new technical assistance, suggests the climatic conditions may have been the predominant factor. (See Chapter 6 for further discussion of the IPM efforts in Choluteca.)

In spite of the respite from pest problems, small farmers once again found themselves unable to escape the consequences of the crisis. The bumper harvests came at a time when market prices for melons were extremely low. Even with higher yields, some producers reportedly did not earn enough to recover their production costs, and many were unable to meet their debt repayment schedules for the second or third consecutive year (Noe Pino and Perdomo 1991). Representatives from

Crehsul and other small producers went to the Honduran government development bank, Banadesa, in an effort to renegotiate their loans. Banadesa responded by declaring that it would no longer extend loans to small producers in the melon sector. USAID stepped in and bought back a portion of the small producers' debt from the bank, but Banadesa continued to resist ventures with small-scale melon producers.

Many small producers faced a difficult future. With limited access to credit, it is hard for small producers to garner the resources necessary to begin the next planting, and with an already heavy debt burden, they will experience even more difficulty in finding new financing for other crops. As one farmer observed, such an option is no longer viable anyway, since "they can't pay their melon debts with corn" (Noe Pino and Perdomo 1991:41). In effect, the smaller earnings gained from corn production are unlikely to generate enough surplus, even over several years, to repay the large loans taken out to grow melons.

The ecological disruption caused by pesticides and the consequent array of pest problems, even when temporarily abated, continued to undermine the economic viability of small melon producers, and shrinking credit markets interacted with the pest problems to create formidable obstacles to small producers. In the case of Honduran melons, it appears that pesticides fueled a full-blown crisis similar to that seen in the Dominican Republic. Also similar to the Dominican case, the small-scale producers appear to have suffered disproportionately more than the rest of the producers, adding to the evidence that social inequity should be included on the list of hazards accompanying chemical technology.

The Guatemalan Industry's Response to the Pesticide Crisis

The renewal of pesticide-driven crises did not go unnoticed among development planners and nontraditional exporters. By the late 1980s several countries were addressing pesticide-related problems. The most ambitious efforts were in Guatemala, which USAID and the pesticide industry considered a priority for their development agendas.[6]

The problems of the Guatemalan nontraditional sector were similar to those seen in the Dominican Republic, Honduras, and elsewhere, including increasing pesticide use, pest problems, and rejections of shipments to the United States because of illegal pesticide residues. In response, USAID's Regional Office for Central America and Panama, in collaboration with PROEXAG, a USAID-funded agency created to provide technical assistance in the production and marketing of nontraditionals, began focusing on reducing pesticide problems. Working closely with the primary exporter and large-producer association in Guatemala, the Gremial de Exportadores de Productos No Tradicionales, development planners organized a variety of workshops, meetings, and field visits, including sessions with EPA and FDA officials, meetings with Guatemalan government and private-sector representatives, and visits and consultancies by various international specialists in pest control and pesticide use, in an effort to gain some control over pesticide use in the sector.

It appears that these concerted efforts have begun to pay off, at least in some areas. The best indicator of a change in pesticide use and pesticide problems can be seen in the changing pattern of violations of FDA residue standards found in shipments of Guatemalan produce to the United States (Table 5-1). Guatemala followed a pattern similar to that of the Dominican Republic. An alarming 27.3 percent of Guatemalan shipments failed FDA inspection in 1990, but the following year the violation rate took a surprising drop to 6.6 percent. Although a variety of factors contributed to this shift, the increasing attention to the pesticide problem and the extensive technical support provided by USAID played an important role in the change.

Yet it is not clear that the extra attention to residues benefited small-scale producers. It appears that at least a portion of the measures to resolve this problem actually undermined the prospects for small producers in Guatemalan nontraditional development. In order to control pesticide use at the production level, some exporters abandoned the satellite system and turned to plantations, as they had in the Honduran melon sector, or to contract farming, relying on fewer and larger producers under close supervision by company technicians.

This transition to more directly controlled farm production was fueled not only by residue concerns but also by other considerations in the international market, including USDA quarantine restrictions against importation of produce containing various insect pests and plant diseases, and cosmetic standards, grading, and quality controls established by the USDA and U.S. importers. By reducing the number of growers they worked with, increasing the technical assistance they offered, and in many cases providing pesticides directly to producers, exporters were better equipped to meet U.S. residue standards and other regulatory or market requirements.

Nontraditional crops in Guatemala are at various stages of the transition from satellite farming, in which companies of a variety of sizes could thrive, to structures with stricter production controls dominated by larger, well-resourced companies with fewer growers. The Guatemalan melon industry appears to have effectively completed this transition. During the 1970s and early 1980s, many small and medium-sized melon growers produced through cooperatives or farmed independently, producing for exporters or selling their harvests to coyotes, who in turn sold to exporting operations. By the end of the 1980s, transnational corporations and large national operators dominated melon production and export. Those small farmers who continued to produce in the melon sector did so under contract to the exporters. As contract farmers, melon growers operated under relatively elaborate written agreements with exporters, and they received technical packages such as seed, fertilizers, pesticides, and regular visits by company technicians.

Melon producers that remained independent were gradually squeezed out of the market. Exporters had large quantities of melons that were not up to export grades, which they sold on the local market, driving the local price down and eliminating the domestic market as a profitable option for small and independent producers. Exporters further squeezed independent farmers by refusing to buy produce not grown under contract. With the increasing concentration and control of land by the melon companies, and the absence of local markets, small farmers found their options shrinking.[7]

The shift to increasing control of melon production did not stop with the implementation of stricter contract farming. With the onset of pesticide-related problems in the late 1980s, control-conscious exporters bought or rented greater areas of land and shifted from satellite production to estate or plantation farming. A few former producers, along with others such as former agricultural technicians, were hired to manage melon fields that were now company property. These producer-employees received supplies from the company and worked under direct company supervision. They were paid a percentage of the harvest, after deduction of input costs, at a rate set by the company.

A survey of 148 nontraditional farmers and thirteen exporters suggested that the pesticide problems contributing to structural change in melons may also be occurring in other nontraditional crops (Hoppin 1991). The study concluded that the relationship between exporter and grower was an important determinant of pesticide practices. Growers associated with companies having better resources and extensive U.S. contacts used pesticides in ways less likely to result in violations of U.S. residue limits than did members of cooperatives or the more independent growers under the satellite farming structure. Similarly, a more recent survey of Guatemalan melon producers found that escalating pesticide use correlated inversely with farm size, with smaller farmers using increasing amounts of pesticides in recent years, while larger farmers reduced their pesticide use (Figure 5-4).

Other crops appear to be going through pesticide-induced structural

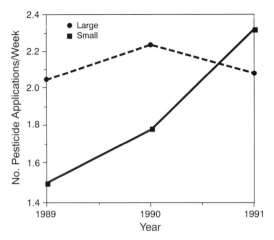

Figure 5-4 Pesticide Use on Melons in Guatemala. Large Farms
(>3.5 mz) vs. Small Farms (<3.5 mz). SOURCE: Conroy et al. forthcoming.

change. Michael Carter, an agricultural economist from the University
of Wisconsin who has been studying nontraditional agriculture in the
Guatemalan highlands, recently reported that ALCOSA, a major proces-
ser and exporter of nontraditional crops, "purged" all the small farmers
with whom it had contracted for production of broccoli. According to
Carter, "FDA was pressuring large exporters on pesticide residues, in-
sisting on a higher degree of quality control. This left exporters with
two alternatives: To grow their own, or to give contracts exclusively to
large farmers" (Peter Rosset, personal communication).

ALCOSA's contract provisions regulating pesticide use among these
farmers had not been effective. The company was faced with testing
each farmer's harvest—2,500 in all—before processing and packaging it
with other broccoli, to eliminate contamination of the products being
exported to the United States. Instead, ALCOSA decided to abandon large
numbers of small farmers who had come to depend on broccoli farming
for their livelihood.

Snow peas are another crop with significant potential pesticide problems. Some have argued that snow pea production is most efficient
when carried out on small plots managed by small farmers, and therefore its promotion has been an effective development strategy for generating economic benefits among poor highland farmers (vonBraun et al.
1989). Yet a survey of snow pea growers in the Guatemalan highlands
found these producers to have significantly higher risk of violating U.S.
residue standards than growers of other nontraditional crops, with snow

pea producers using on average 4.3 prohibited chemicals per season and respecting the intervals between final pesticide application and harvest of the crop for only 37 percent of the chemicals used (Hoppin 1991:192).

The effect of pesticide problems on the structure of the Guatemalan snow pea sector is still unclear. The sector continues to be characterized by a variety of forms of production, with one of the largest exporters of snow peas producing and marketing as a cooperative and another still purchasing snow peas from independent growers through the more traditional satellite system. Yet a third major exporter contracts with only three large producers, in striking contrast to the sector's traditional image as the bastion of small producers, and a possible indicator of future trends in this sector.

The evidence suggests that pesticide-generated crises may yet contribute to land concentration and displacement of small producers in the development of nontraditional agricultural exports. Concentration appears to be occurring more generally throughout the Central American nontraditional sector, as Figure 5-5 indicates. How much of this concentration can be attributed to pesticides remains unclear, but the

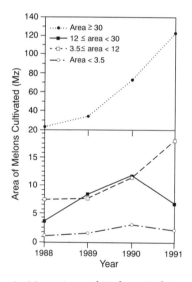

Figure 5-5   Change in Mean Area of Melons Cultivated on Farms of Various Sizes in Guatemala, El Salvador, Honduras, and Costa Rica. Note change in scale in vertical axis. Repeated measures ANOVA showed significant effects of size class ($P<0.001$), year ($P<0.001$), and the interaction between size class and year ($P<0.001$). 1 mz = 0.7 ha. SOURCE: Conroy et al. forthcoming.

evidence from the Dominican Republic, Honduras, and Guatemala indicates that at least in those countries where in-depth case studies of pesticide-generated problems were performed, the agrochemical technology has driven the development of economies of scale biased against the continued participation of smaller producers.[8]

Exporter and Transnational Mobility in the Face of Crisis

There is a final dimension to the relationships among pesticides, ecological crisis, and social change in the nontraditional sector that raises still more questions about the ability of the new development strategy, through its continued emphasis on chemical-intensive farming, to reverse the pattern of increasingly inequitable distribution of the benefits of development that characterized preceding development efforts. It centers on the decidedly different responses of large-scale, transnational operations in comparison with smaller producers when faced with widespread problems. Large-scale operations have encountered many of the same ecological conditions seen in the smaller-scale production units, but the larger operations have often been better equipped to respond to these problems or to survive their effects when they reach a critical stage.[9]

One study of the factors characterizing successful melon production throughout Central America found that the ability to learn over time, to weather the "school of hard knocks," was the key to survival in the melon industry (Byrnes 1989). Among other factors, successful entrepreneurs generally needed four to five years of experience to learn the necessary lessons to assure their success. While the study commended the entrepreneurial spirit of successful farmers, it also acknowledged that the ability to learn was highly dependent upon economic resources. Most of the successful cases described in the study were relatively large producers with access to significant financial resources and were usually integrated into transnational production and marketing structures. All but one were U.S. or British investors.

The larger production units had the resources to survive periodic problems. For example, several contracted international technical assistance to develop measures for controlling melon plant viruses as well as other advanced pest-control techniques to deal with the pest problems on their farms. Large transnational units often shared experiences as new pest problems and control measures developed. In the case of Costa Rica, melon production grew to levels rivaling those of Honduras in only three years, in contrast to the fifteen-year development of the Honduran melon industry (Byrnes 1989). This rapid success was attributed in part to the sharing of information and experience within transnational operations and to the ability of larger Costa Rican producers to contract with international technicians.

Transnational operations also reduced their risk exposure through control of the export and marketing phases of nontraditional agriculture and through contract farming, which allowed them to avoid significant investment in land, infrastructure, and fixed capital (Barry 1987 : 126). Even estate farming was a relatively low-risk venture when land was rented and other capital expenditures were kept low. Transnational operations maintained considerable flexibility in the face of volatile conditions associated with the ecological disruption in the nontraditional sector. Their flexibility allowed them to integrate the crisis-generating capacity of pesticide technology into their production and investment schemes. As indicated in a recent study of investment opportunities in Honduran nontraditional agriculture, melon production has a relatively short period of productivity, as little as five years in a particular site (Tabora 1990) (Table 5-4).[10] Pest problems are the primary factor leading to this short period of return (Murray 1991). Investors having access to such investment profiles are aware that pest problems will likely begin to reduce the return on their investment after a relatively predictable number of years and can plan accordingly.

For example, in Mexico's melon sector, where pest problems have left various melon-producing zones in crisis, exporters acknowledged that they anticipated escalating pest problems and incorporated such losses into their investment strategy (Lopez 1990). Industry representatives in the Autlán Valley reportedly planned for a seven-year production cycle in a particular community or agricultural zone because of pest problems and because related economic and production problems for small farmers led to rising discontent among their producers. Instead of reinvesting locally (the multiplier effect touted by development planners), exporters

Table 5-4   Investment Prospects for Selected
Nontraditional Crops

Crop	Annual investment per hectare	Investment recovery in years	Productive years
Avocado	$3,077	10	50+
Pineapple	$16,006	8	15
Sesame	$1,287	5	5+
Melon	$5,673	2	5

SOURCE: Tabora 1990.

invested profits in new regions of Mexico in order to have production sites available as the anticipated ecological disruption, economic crisis, and social unrest emerged.[11] The vacating exporters left diminished economic opportunities in their wake, potentially exacerbating social inequity.

Even where such planning did not occur, investors, exporters, and transnational producers with limited capital at risk at times simply abandoned communities or entire countries when the crises emerged. Particularly where production was organized through satellite farming, some exporters maintained considerable flexibility through relatively low fixed capital investments. When problems reached critical proportions, these operations had little incentive to remain in existing locales.

The example of the Dominican Republic is again instructive. When the oriental vegetable sector collapsed under the combined weight of pesticide residues and pesticide-resistant pests, exporters took quick steps to overcome at least their own misfortune. Of the dozen or so major exporters, most were Asian investors who ventured as little as $150,000 in their oriental vegetable enterprises. With few local ties and limited capital at risk, these investors closed down their operations and abandoned the Dominican Republic "virtually overnight" (Raynolds 1991 : 16). Many moved to nearby countries like Jamaica, where they set up new operations to export oriental vegetables. For the moment, these exporters were likely free of problems with the FDA, since shipments are detained only after repeated sampling of imports shows violations, and probably free of ecological problems as well, since the new export crops are commonly introduced on lands previously dedicated to less chemical-intensive farming. Left in their wake were two thousand to three thousand satellite farmers whose options and prospects were considerably less favorable than those of the exporters.

As problems grew in the Azua Valley melon and tomato fields of the Dominican Republic, some of the largest transnational operations in the country chose a similar option. Chiquita, one of the leading melon exporters in the Caribbean Basin, abandoned the Azua Valley before the start of the 1990–1991 season, motivated not only by the pesticide problems but also by frustration with the Dominican government's response to the problems and to a variety of other obstacles to nontraditional export development (Murray and Hoppin 1992).[12] The company's move also contributed to severe economic hardship for thousands of rural laborers in Azua.

A leading representative for the melon exporters in Honduras demonstrated that large-scale operators in that country had also developed this flexible strategy, apparently learning from the experience of the melon exporters of Mexico. While bemoaning the prospect of a continued crisis in Cholutecan melon production, he candidly observed, "Like the Mexicans, we may have to move if the problem isn't solved. We are currently looking into some disease-free zones in Nicaragua. If we have to, we can move these packing sheds and equipment in two days" (Murray 1991).

To the transnational investor, such consequences may not be entirely negative. A crisis, once brought under control by state or market forces, may lead to new investment opportunities. With the economic collapse of a particular crop or agricultural system, land prices are likely to decline, and as unemployment rises, wages also are likely to become depressed, conditions these large-scale operations are well situated to exploit. For example, the rise of melons in Choluteca was predicated in part on the previous crisis in Honduran cotton production. With the collapse of cotton, many farmers went bankrupt and unemployment soared, pushing down land value and wages. These in turn became an important part of Choluteca's "comparative advantages" of cheap land and labor, which were touted by development agencies (USAID 1990) and industry sources (Zind 1990) encouraging investors to join in the development of nontraditionals. The cotton crisis set the stage for the next round of ecologically destructive and socially inequitable development.

Conclusion

The pesticide-related problems emerging from the latest round of development based on export agriculture have the capacity to generate renewed ecological crises, albeit on a somewhat more localized or sectoral scale than was the case with Central American cotton. These ecological crises have in turn fueled economic and social problems, including land concentration, farmer and farm laborer impoverishment, and displacement. In effect, current development policies, through their failure to address the ecological disruption inherent in the previous strategies, have led to the re-creation of some of the very economic and social conditions that they were promulgated to overcome.

Meanwhile, large-scale and transnational operations have adapted to many of these ecological problems. They are employing increasingly flexible schemes of capital accumulation that rely on a significant degree of mobility. Although some large producers have adopted better pest-management practices in the face of growing pesticide-related problems, the success of the flexible accumulation strategy suggests that there is little motivation for many of these operations to seek more ecologically sound or locally beneficial production systems. It is likely that this situation will persist as long as these interests can maintain relatively low capital risk and have continually new investment opportunities. Unbridled market competition, which remains the rallying cry of U.S. and international development planners, will compel these operators to pursue short-term profits at the expense of sustainability. In the given economic climate, this will undoubtedly remain the case as one government in the region after another courts transnational investors, with considerable encouragement from the various development institutions, in pursuit of desperately needed investment capital.

Although flexible accumulation schemes do not hold out much promise for a resolution of pesticide problems or other ecologically and socially destructive dimensions to the development process, there have been significant efforts to alter the historic pattern of chemical-intensive agriculture in the region's export sector. The next chapter analyzes the most important aspects of these efforts and the prospects they offer for a resolution to the crisis-generating tendencies of current development strategies.

6

The Search for Solutions: Integrated Pest Management

One of my earliest insights into pesticide problems in Latin America came from a presentation on Nicaragua's Integrated Pest Management (IPM) program, made by U.S. entomologist Sean Swezey at the 1982 founding meeting of the Pesticide Action Network of North America in San Francisco. At the time, the extensive efforts and impressive accomplishments of the Nicaraguan program seemed promising and exciting. During the subsequent decade I had the opportunity to work closely with Dr. Swezey and others pursuing IPM in various parts of Latin America. I came to realize that the pursuit of such alternative farming strategies was far more difficult than it appeared. In many cases, as this chapter argues, the promise and the reality of IPM have remained far apart. Still, it is in these alternative visions that much of the hope for resolving the pesticide problem resides. The past two decades of IPM ventures in the region can illuminate both the opportunities and the obstacles involved in the search for solutions to the pesticide problem.

The Advent of an Alternative Strategy

The repeated crises that beset chemical-intensive agriculture soon led to a quest for more viable and sustainable production strategies. But export agriculture in the postwar era was already deeply entrenched in the Green Revolution's strategy of yield maximization through high technology. In addition, chemical-intensive farming had become part of the foundation of Central America's socioeconomic structure, which was dependent on agroexports. Consequently, the search for solutions to the pesticide-driven ecological disruption and the ensuing socioeconomic problems was heavily conditioned by the forces set in motion by the chemical revolution.

Efforts to overcome the pesticide problems were occurring in several parts of the world during this period. In the 1950s, several important research reports published in the U.S. established the usefulness of "integrated pest control," which subsequently came to be known as integrated pest management (Hansen 1987). As an alternative pest-control strategy, IPM sought to limit or even eliminate the use of pesticides where possible:

> The IPM philosophy makes maximum use of naturally occurring insect controls, using biological, environmental, cultural, and le-

gal methods in a complementary fashion. IPM holds the use of chemical tools to a minimum—they are used only when indicated by a careful survey of the insect populations in the field under consideration. Insect populations are continuously monitored, and control measures are based on specifically calculated economic thresholds or levels of damage, rather than mere pest presence or calendar date. The production/input ratio is maximized within the ecological and social constraints of the environment. (Swezey et al.1986:30)

An early proponent of IPM, Ray Smith from the University of California, sought to demystify the new approach, which was often seen as an esoteric philosophy appropriate for the laboratories and test plots of the research scientists. Smith described IPM as follows: "It's old traditional agriculture with a little bit of sophistication added in" (Bull 1982:139). Smith, along with others,[1] was particularly interested in developing IPM for Third World settings, where research and technological development capacities were limited.

One of the earliest examples of IPM implementation in Latin America occurred in the Cañete Valley of Peru. In 1956, cotton producers began using a range of IPM cultural control methods, legal methods (i.e., banning most organochlorine pesticides), and biological controls in response to pesticide-generated pest problems (Barducci 1972). Their efforts were successful in retrieving the Peruvian cotton sector from virtual collapse. After that early indicator of the potential for IPM in the developing world, another case began to take shape in Central America a decade later. It remains one of the most impressive examples both of the potential for IPM in a Third World setting and of the array of obstacles to its sustained implementation.

Nicaragua: Heading Off the Cotton Crisis

Nicaragua was the first and essentially the only country to respond to the emerging ecological crisis in Central American cotton production in a systematic manner. The Nicaraguan cotton sector was the most advanced in the region, not only in terms of its size and regional economic significance but also in terms of its technological development (ICAITI 1977). Consequently, it was not surprising that this country also took the lead in innovative efforts to overcome the emerging problems. A range of institutional measures was initiated in the mid-1960s after the onset of the first major pest and pesticide-related downturn in the cotton economy. In 1966, the Nicaraguan government formed the National Cotton Commission (Comisión Nacional de Algodón, CONAL) to coordinate responses to various problems in the cotton sector. The following year a cotton research station (Centro de Experimentación de Algodón, CEA) was created with assistance from the government of France. At about the same time, a USDA representative began working with the Nicaraguan Ministry of Agriculture (Ministerio de Agricultura y Ganaderia) to promote better controls of pesticide use after the USDA had rejected more than three hundred thousand pounds of boneless beef contaminated with DDT (Hansen 1987 : 110).

Then, in 1969 the FAO sent a team of specialists to begin devising an IPM strategy for Nicaraguan cotton production. The FAO had begun promotion of IPM several years before (Dinham 1991), and the Nicaraguan effort became one of the early projects pursued by the agency. The project developed in the ensuing four years concentrated largely on reorienting pest control practices through research and technician training. Demonstration plots were established where pest and beneficial insect populations could be studied. By monitoring the development of insect populations, the project developed pest control responses that emphasized nonchemical and low-chemical agronomic practices in an effort to reduce ecological disruption while maintaining or improving cotton yields.

The program called for extensive training of field technicians in scouting and sampling techniques. Scouting was considered a critical element in reducing the high rate of pesticide use (ICAITI 1977). In addition, technicians were taught more ecologically and economically rational tactics such as the use of "economic thresholds," which, contrary to the total-eradication paradigm in use at the time, demonstrated that certain levels of pests and pest damage could be tolerated and were economically preferable to the direct costs of pesticide applications and the indirect costs of ecological damage. This tactic was in part intended to curb the reliance on calendar spraying of pesticides over large tracts of land. By promoting pesticide applications in specific locations within a cotton field, determined by pest population surveys, technicians could reduce pesticide use and restore some semblance of ecological balance.

A graduate program in IPM was also initiated in 1971 at the National Autonomous University of Nicaragua in León, and by the mid-1970s a series of short courses were offered to field technicians to promote the IPM techniques and strengthen the human resource base of the IPM effort (Swezey et al. 1986). In addition, experiments with the release of parasitic wasps (*Trichogramma* spp.) and promotion of the use of microbial pesticides and other biological control agents were initiated during the same period (FAO 1990b : 3).

The benefits of IPM began to be seen almost immediately. Pesticide applications, which had averaged 28 per season during 1967–1968, fell to 21.7 (range 14 to 30) in 1970–1971 in commercial plots (Swezey and Faber 1988 : 58). In project test plots, applications were reduced to 18 per season by 1971–1972 (Falcon and Smith 1973). Aided by favorable rainfall, Nicaragua attained its highest yields on record, nearly six thousand pounds of seed cotton per hectare in the 1971–1972 season, while reducing pesticide use by a third, to just under one hundred pounds per hectare (Swezey et al. 1986 : 30). Meanwhile, in the absence of comparable IPM efforts, El Salvador and Guatemala were applying an average of 158.4 and 165 pounds of pesticides per hectare, respectively, by 1974 (Swezey and Faber 1988 : 59).

In 1974–1975, average applications in commercial Nicaraguan plots had declined to a low of 19.2 per season, which the CONAL attributed to the widespread adoption of IPM techniques (Swezey and Faber 1988). In 1975, the FAO also began financing trap-cropping experiments as an additional dimension to the IPM project. Trap cropping left small patches of cotton plants standing after the harvest while the rest of the fields were plowed under. These plants served as traps where boll weevils concentrated in the absence of other food sources during the off-season. By spraying these small patches and keeping weevil populations down, the tactic sought to prolong the period during the following growing season in which the pest population remained below the economic threshold that warranted pesticide application, thereby delaying the use of pesticides. This in turn reduced the overall volume of chemicals applied in a season.

Trap cropping was aimed at the continued, relatively heavy insecticide use required for boll weevil control. Of the eighteen pesticide applications made in test plots during 1971–1972, twelve to fifteen were directed at boll weevils (FAO 1990b : 3). In commercial fields, boll weevil control accounted for approximately 80 percent of the pesticides used (Daxl et al. 1990). Trap cropping was seen as an innovative tactic that could reduce pesticide use through reliance on increasing human resources, particularly through the use of scouting.

Dr. Robert Metcalf of the University of Illinois, one of the leading authorities on pesticide problems and IPM, has referred to the year 1976 as the beginning of "the era of IPM" in the United States, when scientists, agricultural officials, and farmers began to recognize, albeit in limited fashion, that chemical pest control would not provide a long-term solution to their production problems (Hansen 1987 : 35). Ironically, the fortunes of IPM took a strikingly different course at about the same time in Central America.

Following the record profit levels of the 1971–1972 season, cotton hectarage began a dramatic increase in Nicaragua as local and foreign investors continued to pursue the vision of quick fortunes that accompanied the initial cotton boom of the 1950s and 1960s (Table 2-1). Cotton farming more than doubled, reaching 212,000 hectares in 1978.

But the rapid expansion of cotton hectarage quickly exceeded the human resource base being developed through the IPM efforts of national and international agencies. The supply of trained personnel was stretched thin as the government resisted or was unable to make the investments necessary to meet the growing demand for technicians. Also, given the historical neglect of smaller cotton producers by the Central Bank and government technical assistance programs (Colburn 1986; Enriquez 1991), the IPM efforts left an important part of the cotton producers completely outside the program. This allowed pest problems to continue to develop and potentially to spread from the smaller farms back into those areas covered by IPM technicians.

The shortage of trained personnel did not result in significant economic benefits to the technicians. Technicians' wages remained low as farmers and government policymakers, in keeping with the quick-return vision of the cotton producers, continued to resist paying for the development and maintenance of skilled personnel. Technicians began to take responsibility for larger and larger tracts of land in order to augment their income, reaching an average of one thousand hectares each by the late 1970s (Hansen 1987:117). Consequently, the quality of their field supervision declined. Government-sponsored IPM measures faltered as inadequate funding combined with the expanding area in cotton cultivation to weaken the IPM effort. By 1977 government efforts covered only 13 percent of the total cotton hectarage.

The inability to maintain the human resources necessary for sector-wide IPM was not, however, the only factor undermining the alternative pest control strategy. A serious drought began during the 1972–1973 season and continued for five years, causing lower yields. The drought triggered an outbreak of the cotton whitefly (Bemisia tabaci) in 1973–1974. Severe problems with the cotton leaf miner (Bucculatrix thurberiella) also developed throughout this period, and during 1976 and 1977 Spodoptera, Trichoplusia, and Heliothis all plagued the cotton sector (Hansen 1987:116).

With the declining yields and escalating pest problems, risk-averse cotton producers began to abandon IPM in favor of the quick technological fix promised by pesticides. The shift back to exclusive chemical control was promoted by chemical salespeople who warned farmers of the financial risks posed by pest outbreaks (Swezey and Faber 1988). Chemical company efforts were furthered by the actions of the CEA.

Working closely with chemical-industry technicians and sales personnel, the CEA staff registered and recommended an ever wider range of chemicals. Review of CEA files demonstrated that many chemicals had little supporting data to warrant their registration, and in some instances the data did not suggest that the chemicals were appropriate for the uses to which they were applied (Swezey et al. 1986).

The banks likewise undermined efforts to reduce pesticide use. Rising pesticide prices and declining world market prices for cotton combined to reduce Nicaragua's foreign currency earnings at a time when the entire region was having trouble servicing its soaring debt. In an effort to stimulate foreign exchange earnings, the Nicaraguan banks offered bonuses to producers who exceeded normal yield levels (Swezey and Faber 1988). The bonuses spurred growers to pursue immediate gains through pesticide applications at the expense of longer-term ecological stability. One study of the bonus system found that the higher yields achieved through increased pesticide applications occurred at twice the level of maximum profit from pesticide use (Villagran 1981). It appears that the strategy may have benefited the financial institutions by increasing foreign exchange earnings. Clearly it benefited the chemical companies through increased chemical sales. But the promotion of pesticide use through this bonus system offered dubious benefits, at best, for the producers.

Not surprisingly, technicians began to abandon the IPM tactics. Under pressure from the various forces at work in the cotton sector, 20 percent of the pesticide application recommendations made by the IPM technicians were made solely in response to farmer fears (FAO 1980). In addition, producers reportedly ignored IPM recommendations 25 percent of the time, opting for the recommendations of chemical salespeople and others (FAO 1980; Swezey and Faber 1988). While the number of applications rose only slightly during the 1970s, the dosage of chemicals in each application increased significantly. By the 1977–1978 season, pesticide use reached 174 pounds per hectare as the IPM innovations and the efforts to reduce pesticide use in Nicaraguan cotton collapsed.

Falling cotton prices late in the decade heightened the crisis in the cotton sector. In addition, rising social and political turmoil, which culminated in the Sandinista-led insurrection of 1979, undermined cotton production. Some producers decapitalized and fled the country, while others withheld further investment until the prospects for social and ecological stability improved. In 1979, as the insurrection peaked, cotton hectarage, yields, and profits fell to their lowest levels in twenty years (Hansen 1987:117).

Nicaragua's Second IPM Program

Following the overthrow of the Somoza regime in 1979, the new Sandinista-led government looked to a revitalized cotton sector as a primary source of foreign exchange earnings. The capital generated by cotton, at least in the short term, was seen as an important source of financing for the rebuilding of the devastated national economy. The country was virtually bankrupt, with a $1.6 billion external debt (Booth and Walker 1989:61). The insurrection had resulted in more than fifty thousand deaths (almost 2 percent of the population) and $1.5 billion in property damage. A concerted effort was made to expand the area under cotton production, with an initial target of 100,000 hectares and a five-year goal of 160,000 hectares. The disruption caused by the insurrection made it difficult to mobilize human resources and equipment for the 1980–1981 cotton cycle, but the spring planting still brought 94,000 hectares under cotton cultivation. The aftermath of the conflict continued to undermine the cotton economy through the following year as equipment and personnel shortages led farmers to neglect their fields after the harvest. Failure to plow under the cotton plants left the boll weevil with ample sustenance during the off-season. An unusually moist summer followed, which further benefited the boll weevil, leading to phenomenal population growth and the highest boll weevil densities ever seen in Nicaraguan cotton (Hansen 1987). Pesticide application rates rose to an average of 27 for the 1981–1982 season, representing 26 percent of total production costs (Swezey et al. 1986:32). Losses still amounted to 20 percent of preharvest estimates, worth over $42 million or 16 percent of Nicaragua's foreign exchange earnings from agriculture.

Nicaragua's new government took significant steps, beginning in 1981, to create a more effective IPM program that could sustain the expansion envisioned by economic planners. The new program relied on many of the successful dimensions of the earlier IPM efforts, focusing on the suppression of the boll weevil. The program gave significant attention to the off-season management of cotton lands, including legal requirements that plants be plowed under after the harvest.

The program renewed the emphasis on trap cropping. With financial and technical assistance from West Germany and several other donor countries, the government also expanded experiments in the rearing and use of parasitic wasps and other biological controls, including bacterial pesticides like *Bacillus thuringiensis* (Hansen 1987). The use of bacterial pesticides was particularly appealing to cotton producers because it allowed them to substitute new products for existing chemicals without making major changes in the production process.

More important, the effort sought to involve all the cotton producers, from large to small private producers, cooperatives, and state farms. To assure better technical support, several hundred new technicians were trained to scout and to monitor trap crops in the cotton fields (Swezey et al. 1986). In addition, the national university in León initiated another graduate program in 1981 to replace the moribund program from the early 1970s. It developed a rigorous three-year master's degree in IPM to provide highly skilled personnel for Nicaraguan IPM efforts.

The commitment to human resources accompanied an effort to expand coverage. In 1982, 16,800 hectares were incorporated into an intensive IPM project to maintain six thousand trap crops (Swezey et al. 1986). The results from the first season were mixed, partly because of differences in rainfall between the two zones included in the project (Hansen 1987). But total crop yields were higher than normal, and the combined effect of the IPM controls was impressive, with a savings of $2.93 million in insecticide use and an overall savings of $2.14 million after deductions for the increased labor costs (Swezey et al. 1986:34). In the 1983–1984 season, the project was expanded to include a third zone, incorporating a total of 33,600 hectares. The government adopted Decree 1226 on April 6, 1983, making measures to suppress boll weevils between seasons mandatory for all producers. By 1984, the Nicaraguan IPM program was the largest effort in the region and possibly in all of Latin America. The promise of a major reduction in pesticide use and a commensurate decline in the array of pesticide-related problems throughout the Nicaraguan cotton-growing region seemed to be within reach.

Similar to the experiences of a decade earlier, the initial successes of the IPM program in the 1980s encouraged the Nicaraguan government and growers to expand the cotton sector. In 1983, 116,000 hectares were planted, a two-and-one-half-fold increase over 1980. But the optimism generated by the improvements in cotton production did not take into account the increasingly difficult context in which Nicaragua was pursuing its development goals.

The initial shortages of materials and personnel after 1979 were somewhat offset by new economic aid and technical assistance from a variety of sources around the world.[2] By the mid-1980s those economic resources were becoming more difficult to obtain as the government of the United States became increasingly successful at undermining the Sandinista regime. Materials, fuel, and equipment for agricultural production became even more scarce. With the escalation of the conflict with the contra on Nicaragua's northern and southern borders and the related economic problems, trained IPM technicians also became scarce as they were drafted into national defense activities, left the country in search of better economic opportunities, or fled military draft and the war.[3] Some were even hired by chemical companies to promote pesticides.

In May of 1985, President Reagan placed an embargo on all trade with Nicaragua, making official what had been unofficial for several years. The Inter-American Development Bank withdrew a pending agricultural loan for $156 million, followed by the withdrawal of agricultural development assistance by the government of West Germany, directly undermining the IPM program (Hansen 1987:123). The decline of economic and technical support, when combined with the expansion of cotton production, placed the IPM program once again in the untenable position of trying to maintain support for large-scale activities with inadequate human and material resources. Trap crops were inadequately monitored and maintained. In some cases this resulted in a complete reversal of the intended role of the trap crops, as the untended parcels fostered increases in the off-season boll weevil populations instead of serving as loci for suppressing cotton pests.

Growers and government technicians gave greater emphasis to the use of substitute products like *Bacillus thuringiensis*, preferring to rely on "magic bullets" instead of methods that were more human-resource intensive, like monitoring and scouting. From 1985 through 1987 the IPM program declined until it was little more than a laboratory and test-plot-based project. Efforts to rebuild the program in 1988 and after confronted ever more difficult problems as the Nicaraguan economy virtually collapsed.

With the advent of the government of Violeta Chamorro in 1990, the cotton sector once again was seen as a solution to the disastrous economic problems of the country. The new government and some international development planners looked longingly back to the days before the rise of the Sandinista government, when cotton was king. In a meeting with members of the multilateral aid community in Managua, soon after the elections, the Nicaraguan minister of agriculture presented plans that included a rapid expansion of cotton farming to 180,000 hectares by 1992, projecting that per hectare yields would increase from twenty-eight quintales to forty (personal interview, Peter Rosset, June 4, 1992).

Some U.S. officials were equally enthusiastic about the return of the cotton economy. In what seemed like a parody of a scene from the movie *The Graduate*, in which Mr. Robinson sagely tells a young Dustin Hoffman that the future can be found in one word, "plastics," a U.S. embassy official replied with similar confidence to a visiting scholar's question about the key to Nicaragua's future with another single word: "cotton" (T. W. Walker 1991:119). Other U.S. and international development officials have responded in less sanguine terms, with a recent

FAO report concluding that Nicaragua's cotton economy was in a state of irreversible decline (FAO 1990a). While IPM efforts continue in Nicaragua, they have not assumed a level of importance comparable to the successful phases of the two earlier periods.

In neighboring El Salvador, a cotton IPM project was also undertaken in the late 1980s, with assistance from West Germany and several development organizations. But this program achieved very few measurable results. Salvadorans attributed the lack of a successful IPM program to the effects of the war in the cotton zones of El Salvador, where growers reportedly lost $7 million through crop and machinery destruction (*Salpress* Feb. 12, 1992). But as an FAO evaluation noted, the conflict did not have a similar effect on the promotion of chemical strategies in the same cotton zones (FAO 1990b: 10). Instead, the FAO attributed the absence of effective IPM in that country, as well as in Guatemala, to a continued failure of national governments to commit to developing and sustaining alternatives to chemical pest control. Unphased by the FAO critique, Salvadoran Minister of Agriculture Antonio Cabrales recently announced that the restoration of the nation's cotton production was among the government's goals in the coming years, with forty thousand hectares projected for the 1992 planting (*Salpress* Feb. 12, 1992).

The Spread of IPM to Other Crops

By the 1980s, IPM had failed to make notable inroads on the pesticide problem in Central American cotton. Pesticides remained the primary pest control strategy and continued to generate serious environmental, public health, and production problems. But significant changes were beginning to develop in other agricultural sectors. One of the side benefits of the FAO's initial IPM efforts in Nicaraguan cotton was the writing of the first manuals in Central America promoting the use of IPM in basic grains (Swezey et al. 1986). By the early 1980s experiments were under way in agricultural training and research centers in the region, focusing on smaller-scale production of subsistence and domestic-market crops.

The Panamerican Agricultural School, at Zamorano, Honduras, with funding from USAID, initiated an IPM program in 1983 that supplemented the more traditional agricultural education offered at the school and also provided some local assistance to producers of corn, beans, and cabbage (personal interview, Keith Andrews, Jan. 25, 1992). In 1986 the school established the Crop Protection Department, which gave increasing emphasis to IPM, biological control, and other alternative or pesticide-reduction strategies.

Similarly, experimentation with IPM techniques rose in priority at the Center for Tropical Agriculture Research and Extension (CATIE), in Turrialba, Costa Rica, which was the leading agricultural research center in the region. In 1985 CATIE formally established an IPM project, again focusing primarily on basic grains (personal interview, Joseph Saunders, Jan. 31, 1992). In collaboration with the Central American ministries of agriculture, CATIE assisted local research and demonstration projects and began training ministry technicians and extension agents in the IPM philosophy and techniques. In 1986 CATIE initiated a master's degree program in IPM, and it graduated the first class in 1988.

By the end of the decade, IPM had become so widely recognized in Central American research centers and universities that the former coordinator of CATIE's IPM project in Costa Rica described it as "the dominant paradigm in regional pest control research" (personal communication, Peter Rosset, June 4, 1992). Yet the dominance in research did not translate into dominance in farmer practices. Pesticide use and pesticide problems continued to develop throughout the region during the 1980s. Related health, environmental, and production problems were increasing in basic grains, even as numerous IPM alternatives were being identified. As cotton production and consequently cotton-related pesticide problems declined, similar problems became common in crops produced for local markets (Contreras 1990).

The dissemination of IPM techniques continued to follow the strategy employed by the FAO in cotton a decade earlier. It relied on highly trained technicians working directly with producers or through field technicians. Much of the actual work outside the research centers and farm test plots involved formal courses or seminars for field technicians or producers. The IPM efforts were primarily channeled through government institutions, particularly the applied research and extension services of the ministries of agriculture. These agencies historically had achieved only limited success in reaching farmers. During the economic crisis of the 1980s and the consequent shrinking of the public sector most extension efforts were completely ineffective at reaching the farmers in the region.

The weakness of extension efforts through government institutions was compounded by declining support for IPM from key international agencies. In spite of its leading role in the early development of Central American IPM, the FAO never followed through in the region. In 1974, the FAO formulated its Cooperative Global Programme for the Development and Application of Integrated Pest Control in Agriculture during an ad hoc meeting in Rome of the FAO-UNEP Panel of Experts on Integrated Pest Control. The Global Programme was developed "with the aim to bring IPM to [the] field level through IPM implementing programmes" (Schulten n.d.:2). Two years later, in the fall of 1976, the FAO drafted a proposal for the Latin America Inter-Country Programme for the Development and Application of Integrated Pest Control in Cotton Growing. Building on the FAO's initial efforts, the Latin America Programme started in nine countries, including the leading Central American producers of El Salvador, Nicaragua, and Guatemala. The program was funded by the U.N. Environmental Programme (UNEP) at $420,000.

The program developed national IPM projects and drafted a regional funding proposal for $6.4 million (FAO 1984:10). This request was never funded, and the program terminated in 1985. The efforts to "bring IPM to the field level" never got beyond a series of three regional training courses in cotton IPM and forty-plus scientific presentations in participating countries. The FAO acknowledged several of the weaknesses in its IPM program, including the mistaken assumption that significant funding would be forthcoming for the development of IPM. It also recognized the critical shortage of personnel and the weakness of government extension programs, as well as the power of competing interests: "A serious constraint in many countries was the insufficient level of extension activities, whilst the private sector had an active sales promotion network which contacted regularly the authorities concerned and the farmers, convincing them that frequent and regular use of pesticides is necessary for good yields" (Schulten n.d.:6). The FAO expressed frustration with national government policies, which in many instances continued to subsidize pesticide prices, thus encouraging excessive use of the chemicals.

That combination of factors led the FAO to repeatedly question IPM as an alternative strategy for the developing world in various international meetings (FAO 1988). Only recently has the FAO begun to question whether the top-down, technician-centered extension strategy pursued by the agency might also be responsible for some of the shortcomings.[4] The conventional view of IPM as a technological package delivered by FAO experts has slowly given way to a recognition that more participation by local farmers in both research and promotion of IPM may be crucial for implementing the alternative strategy at the farm level (Schulten n.d.).[5]

IPM and Nontraditional Agriculture

With the emergence of major pesticide problems in the new nontraditional export crops, it was not long before development planners renewed their interest in IPM. If the IPM efforts in cotton a decade earlier were more difficult than planners had anticipated, the task they were facing in the late 1980s was beyond anything they had contemplated.

Instead of working with a single crop like cotton, they faced dozens of different nontraditionals, each with a distinct agroecology and its own particular pest problems, which posed a formidable challenge to researchers and technicians seeking quick palliatives for the emerging problems. Few IPM options were readily available for the new sector. Some of the largest operators in the nontraditional sector employed various IPM techniques or contracted international specialists to develop IPM programs (Murray 1989a, 1991).

IPM strategies frequently required widespread implementation to control various pests. This meant that large numbers of small producers had to participate as well. But the large operators were often reluctant to share their production techniques with their competitors and resisted providing assistance to smaller operators. Nevertheless, they commonly pointed to the small farmers as the source of escalating pest problems. In some cases their complaints were well founded, as small operators failed to plow under postharvest plants, which in turn created reservoirs for pest population growth in the off-season (Murray 1991; Murray et al. 1989).

Prompted largely by FDA rejections of imports contaminated with residues in the late 1980s, as well as by mounting pest resistance in various crops, USAID and other development institutions began exploring potential solutions. In keeping with the commitment to nontraditional exports and the reduction of basic grain production in Central America,[6] USAID's Regional Office for Central America and Panama (ROCAP) began pressuring CATIE to shift resources and research from IPM for basic grains and vegetables for domestic markets to nontraditional crops (personal interviews, anonymous).

CATIE officials and researchers resisted the shift, in part because the institution's mandate was to serve the range of small-farmer interests in the region. Since basic grain production included the vast majority of Central American farmers, this sector remained a priority for CATIE. Given that USAID was a primary source of CATIE's funding, the researchers and technicians found themselves in a difficult position. USAID chose to cut a portion of CATIE's funding in 1992, eliminating much of the institution's education and extension capacity. The move was seen by some CATIE personnel and others as an indication that U.S. planners intended to forge ahead with the narrowly focused agenda for the development of IPM and nontraditional agriculture in Central America, further reducing institutional support and opportunities for producers in the small-scale domestic market and subsistence farmers. CATIE, according to these sources, was but the latest victim of the heavy-handed politics of U.S. planners.

During the same period, USAID increased its funding for the Panamerican Agricultural School, finding an institution more receptive to the agency's promotion of nontraditional exports. In part the Zamorano school's willingness to give greater attention to IPM in nontraditional crops was due to the absence of conflicting demands on the school's resources, as ROCAP provided additional funding for the nontraditional IPM project and the school's other activities continued unimpeded. In addition, most of the school's activities already involved training mid-level field technicians, combined with applied research. Adding new crops to those training and education activities was easier than shifting the focus of CATIE's primary research.

But a pest crisis in Honduras's nontraditional sector was likely the more critical element in Zamorano's choice. The pest explosion in the southern Honduran melon sector of Choluteca (see Chapter 5) during the 1989–1990 season underscored the need for major changes in the sector's chemical-intensive system. With ROCAP funding, Zamorano sent a full-time IPM specialist to assist melon producers in Choluteca. Working with small farmers in Choluteca's largest cooperative, the specialist developed a series of demonstration plots to identify pest problems and test responses. More important, the strategy moved away from the technology-transfer approach, which linked laboratory to test plot (via a technician) to farmer in a top-down manner, the conventional FAO and government approach. Instead, the Choluteca effort gave considerable (although not exclusive) emphasis to techniques based on small-farmer experiences. As the Zamorano specialist, Lorena Lastres, observed, "In this model of work we do not use the conventional experiment stations. Everything is carried out at the farm level" (Barletta and Rueda 1991:24).

A central component of the recent work in the melon IPM project has been the development of a farmer's menu of responses to pest problems. More than forty traditional and nonchemical techniques were identified by small farmers working with the Zamorano technician and were then tested and evaluated by the producers in demonstration plots on their farms. Small farmers now can choose from a range of techniques that they developed and tested themselves. The project is also developing trap cropping, plant barriers to inhibit the entry of pests into melon fields, and other cultural and nonchemical pest-control strategies.[7]

Preliminary results have been encouraging. The 1990–1991 harvest was the largest on record (Figure 5-2). Unusual weather conditions played an important role in reducing pest problems and boosting yields, but some observers give the IPM efforts considerable credit for the improvement in melon production (Barletta and Rueda 1991). At the least, the spreading acceptance of the IPM project among small producers in the zone suggests that this farmer-based approach may be more sustainable than the earlier IPM efforts.

Yet there remain serious obstacles to this project's success as well. From its inception, the project was contemplated as technical assistance sustained by producers, instead of the usual reliance on external and international sources for maintenance of IPM. While many producers supported the idea of an IPM program, few were willing to provide the funds for its execution. ROCAP financed the first efforts, but after considerable pressure, several of the larger producers began contributing their own resources (personal interview, Lorena Lastres). Even so, most support came from several of the largest operations, including the transnationals, who saw the IPM project as one of the few remaining opportunities to contain the explosive pest outbreaks (personal interview, George Garcelón, USAID, Honduras). Crehsul, the largest cooperative of small producers, reportedly is also providing financing to the Zamorano project, but it remains unclear whether the necessary sectorwide support can be established. If effective cooperation and financial support are not sustained, the initial gains in Choluteca may be lost before long.

Conclusion

Repeated crises in Central American agriculture provided the impetus for developing alternative pest-control strategies. IPM projects emerged from the combined efforts of international organizations, the national governments, and agricultural producers. In spite of early successes, the alternative measures failed to replace chemical-intensive farming as the dominant and frequently exclusive means of pest control.

Proponents of chemical pest control were quick to argue that in practical terms, IPM was simply a myth created by researchers and naive or idealistic environmentalists who had little understanding of the realities of Latin American farming.[8] But the failure of IPM to take hold in Latin American farming had more to do with the context in which it was developed, as well as the methods through which it was pursued, than with any inherent weakness in the IPM philosophy.

The strategy behind developing IPM in the region relied heavily on an infrastructure of high-tech human resources. Highly trained researchers and technicians were the key link between the philosophy and its widespread application. In the context of the traditionally weak public sectors of the region and, more important, in the conjunctural context of the decade-long economic crisis and structural adjustment policies that further curtailed state activities, the new strategy was clearly not going to be widely adopted.

The limited effect of the FAO IPM project and related activities exposed a fundamental conceptual flaw in the strategy. Proponents of IPM sought to substitute pest control based on high technology human resources for pest control based on high technology chemicals. A top-down approach for the development and transfer of new technologies was ultimately ineffectual in that setting. As in any top-down system, if the elements at the top become weakened or disappear, nothing remains to sustain the IPM effort below.

The recent development of more participatory, farmer-first, and agro-ecology approaches to IPM suggests a new momentum may be building for an alternative to chemical-intensive farming. Such strategies have made major improvements in other regions of the developing world, such as the FAO's countrywide program in Indonesia (Useem et al. 1992), but this alternative continued to play a minor role in the overall scheme of Central American agriculture in the early 1990s.

It would be misleading to attribute the weakness of IPM to date solely to the structural obstacles posed by Central American tradition and the economic crisis or to the technocratic biases of the IPM proponents. Throughout this period of increasing attention to IPM there was a competing vision of how to overcome the pesticide crises that dominated the development discourse. While this alternative vision provided the hope of relief from at least some aspects of the pesticide problem, it also served as an obstacle to the transition to an IPM strategy. The next chapter examines this competing vision.

7

The Search for Solutions: The Safe-Use Paradigm

During the mid-1980s, I dedicated the bulk of my energies to developing the CARE Nicaragua Pesticide Health and Safety Program. This effort involved a series of projects, described below, which primarily sought to reduce pesticide hazards in a context of continued pesticide use. I believed at the time that such efforts were necessary to protect workers and the public until IPM and other alternative strategies became established.

Gradually during this period, and much more since my departure from Nicaragua in 1988, I grew suspicious of the long-term effect of safe-use efforts. I came to realize that the dedication of energy and resources to this strategy, while achieving some reduction of pesticide hazards, was not complementing the greater efforts to develop alternative pest control strategies. Instead, safe use was being pursued in lieu of alternatives.

Further, I began to conclude that safe-use measures were reducing pesticide hazards far less than many had hoped and many more were claiming. This was in part attributable to the continued and even increasing use of pesticide technology that the safe-use strategy indirectly (and directly) fostered. This paradoxical effect is an important dynamic of the safe-use paradigm and its role in Latin American development.

Chemical-industry representatives, many agricultural technicians and policymakers, and other proponents of chemical-intensive pest control frequently argued that pesticides, when used according to the manufacturer's instructions, were not inherently more hazardous than many technologies with which we come in contact every day. This assumption, for example, was implicit in the pesticide registration system of the EPA and other related regulatory programs. After eliminating chemicals manifesting hazards beyond a limit of acceptable risk, the agency would register pesticides for specific uses. Labels with instructions for safe and proper use were required for product containers. The assumption was that these products could and would be used as indicated. The problems they generated were considered the result of improper or indiscriminate use, which in turn was seen as the consequence of inadequate training and education, combined with a failure to enforce effective regulatory controls.

The development of strategies promoting the safe, rational, and efficient use of pesticides was a logical expression of the faith in the viability of the technology. Such faith, and these strategies, dominated efforts to resolve pesticide problems. As the efforts to adopt integrated and alternative pest management strategies faltered, or at least lagged behind the various problems, the safe-use paradigm came to be seen as the most viable and immediate response to pesticide problems. Improving user knowledge of proper chemical mixing, application, and storage procedures, as well as the promotion of personal protection and hygiene measures, superseded more-complex efforts to educate users about alternative pest control and to reduce pesticide use as a means of reducing pesticide problems. After more than a decade of pursuing safe-use efforts, it appears that this strategy may have promised a great deal more than it delivered.

The Chemical Industry and Safe Use

Popular pressure was building throughout the 1970s and into the 1980s for fundamental changes in pesticide regulation. Groups like the International Organization of Consumer Unions, OXFAM, and the Pesticide Action Network were making demands in international forums for changes in the way pesticides were produced, marketed, and used in the developing world.

The pesticide industry became more active in the international policy arena as popular pressures increased. Indicative of the industry's response to critics was one chemical company executive's acknowledgment of what had become an undeniable truth for many opponents of chemical-intensive agriculture: "We have not been completely successful in harmonizing pesticide technology with the cultural forces and values of our own society. It is proving infinitely more difficult to achieve a successful accommodation of pesticide technology with the cultures and economies of the lesser developed countries" (Bull 1982: 87). Industry interests focused significant attention on the international development organizations, particularly the FAO, where agribusiness and the petrochemical industry had historically exercised considerable influence (Dinham 1991; Sesmou 1991). The FAO had formed a pesticide program as early as 1959 and had been a strong proponent of increased pesticide and fertilizer use to stimulate food production in the developing world (Dinham 1991).

In the mid-1960s, the Groupement International des Associations Nationales de Fabricants de Produits Agrochimiques (GIFAP) was created to lobby on behalf of the international chemical industry. Roughly half of GIFAP's funding came from the National Agricultural Chemical Association (NACA), the U.S. chemical industry's lobbying arm (Boardman 1986: 45). GIFAP began working closely with FAO representatives, primarily through the Industry Cooperative Program (ICP) within the FAO (Chapin and Wasserstrom 1983).

By the early 1970s the FAO and GIFAP were collaborating on a series of seminars to promote "new and better ways" to distribute and use pesticides in the developing world as industry and the FAO's consensual vision of safe use began to take shape (Dinham 1991 : 63). The FAO's faith in chemical pest control was reaffirmed in 1974 at the World Food Conference, in which the FAO pledged to help increase developing countries' access to pesticides and fertilizers in order to stimulate food production. Even though the chemical industry's insider relationship with the FAO was challenged by various public interest groups, leading to the disbanding of the ICP in the mid-1970s, the pesticide lobby continued to have access to and influence in the agency throughout the 1970s and 1980s.

The FAO began promoting safe-use strategies more vigorously in the early 1980s to head off challenges from the UNEP and WHO to its primary jurisdiction over pesticide issues within the United Nations institutional structure (Paarlberg 1991 : 18). In 1981 the agency's director-general proposed the International Code of Conduct on the Distribution and Use of Pesticides after some nongovernmental organizations (NGOs) raised such an idea amid charges that both industry and the UN had ignored the mounting evidence of major pesticide problems in the developing world.

GIFAP and the individual pesticide companies similarly joined the FAO in developing the code of conduct in a preemptive effort to avoid more institutional involvement in the international pesticide market. They emphasized such measures as the need for more appropriate labeling of pesticide containers to provide information on application rates and user protection. In addition, they gave considerable attention to the need for technician and user training.

The FAO reasserted its jurisdiction over the pesticide issue in the international arena during the ensuing five years through the drafting and redrafting of the code. NGO activists worked closely with the FAO in the development of the code. OXFAM's David Bull was contracted to write the first draft, leading some critics to charge the agency with co-opting the opposition (Paarlberg 1991 : 22). Indeed, many of Bull's proposals were removed at the insistence of GIFAP and the FAO during the ten revisions that occurred between 1982 and 1985. In addition, the FAO and GIFAP succeeded, over repeated challenges, in maintaining the voluntary nature of the code's implementation and enforcement in the final version, which was adopted in 1986.

At the same time, industry interests and similar-minded FAO staffers continued to challenge alternative strategies such as IPM. Even as the FAO was promoting the few IPM projects in the developing world, major policy statements from various committees within the agency challenged the applicability of IPM (Schulten n.d.). Industry's opposition to IPM was in part due to an obvious self-interest in the promotion of products, but it was also driven by the fear (not totally without foundation) that once IPM techniques were found to be effective, they would be used to support more radical challenges to the continuation of chemical pest control (NACA 1981 : 1).

Safe Use in Central America

Industry-sponsored seminars on the safe use of pesticides began in the 1970s in Central America and increased considerably during the 1980s. Improved product labels, various training materials, and a wide range of posters, pamphlets, and advertisements addressing how to use pesticides properly and the benefits to be gained from so doing were distributed by GIFAP and individual chemical companies during the 1980s. Pesticide company representatives generally outnumbered the government and nongovernment agency representatives in regional conferences convened to analyze pesticide problems and possible solutions, such as the First Seminar on Environment and Development with Emphasis on Agrochemicals, in Guatemala City in 1986, and the Seminar on Problems Associated with the Use of Pesticides, at the International Institute for Cooperation in Agriculture in Costa Rica a year later. Similarly, the chemical companies were traditionally the primary, if not exclusive, source of pesticide-related training and information in countries such as Guatemala (Campos 1986 : 19).

Companies like Ciba Geigy, Bayer, and ICI conducted safe-use seminars for government and private technicians. These seminars usually combined the promotion of specific products marketed by each company with the more general messages of safe or rational use of pesticides. In addition, company technicians and sales personnel frequently visited farms and provided a wide variety of inducements to use their products and to use them as instructed. Promotional incentives offered by the companies for pesticide users ranged from hats and T-shirts bearing the company or product logos to fancy dinners and trips to conferences for farm managers and government officials.

During the same period, CARE International in Nicaragua initiated a somewhat different project, the Pesticide Health and Safety Program (Murray 1989b). It focused on reducing the high incidence of pesticide poisoning in the Nicaraguan cotton sector. Similar to the chemical-company efforts, CARE's safe-use activities concentrated on training pesticide users, combined with considerable attention to community education. Unlike the industry's training, CARE's made no effort to defend or promote chemical-intensive pest control. Instead, health monitoring data generated through a collaboration between program personnel and the Ministry of Health were regularly publicized through the local media, in addition to being part of worker training, in an effort to raise popular awareness of the scope of health and environmental problems linked to pesticides.

Workers were trained in safety measures while being encouraged and assisted in the organization of ongoing workplace safety committees (Weinger and Lyons 1992). These committees were designed to follow up on training and to help define worker and government measures for improvements in agricultural health and safety. In addition, the program focused on the use and availability of personal protective equipment, such as respirators, rubber gloves and boots, hats and coveralls, along with personal hygiene practices, including the construction and use of showers and wash facilities. Similar to several company efforts, the CARE program provided closed-system mixing and loading equipment to farms handling large volumes of pesticides and assisted in the design and construction of infrastructure for improved hygiene and safety. From 1984 to 1988, the program installed closed systems in thirty workplaces and trained and annually monitored the health of up to five thousand farm workers and others at risk from pesticide exposure (Cole et al. 1988; Murray 1989b; Weinger and Lyons 1992).

CARE began shifting its focus to producers of basic grains near the end of the decade as cotton production and pesticide use in Nicaragua declined and economic crisis shook the region. CARE received a $2 million, five-year grant from the Norwegian government in 1989, at which point the program began to emphasize alternative pest control. This shift was based on the conclusion of program personnel that greater reductions in pesticide-related illness could be achieved by reducing pesticide use than by promoting health and safety measures alone.[1] Over time, the program has integrated health and safety training with on-farm IPM development, while maintaining the health surveillance system established in the Ministry of Health in León. The CARE program continues to be the largest NGO effort in the region to develop alternative strategies for resolving pesticide problems. In addition, the Pan American Health Organization (PAHO) of the WHO is about to initiate a ten-year program to expand and adapt León's health surveillance system and create a seven-country system of pesticide-illness surveillance and response. It appears that CARE may reduce its support of illness surveillance as the PAHO program develops and concentrate its resources on the expansion of IPM.

In June 1991, GIFAP initiated a major program to implement the safe-use strategy. With a commitment of $1,059,000 from the international office in Brussels, GIFAP's regional organization, FECCOPIA, initiated a multifaceted, three-year pilot project in Guatemala designed to raise user and public awareness of the proper methods for pesticide use (personal interview, Anarco Garcia, Project Director, FECCOPIA, Jan. 17, 1992). A similar pilot project has been designed for Kenya and Thailand to test the strategy in different cultural and geographical settings.

The new project focuses on a variety of training and education measures, as well as developing and distributing new types of personal protective equipment and creating a toxic-waste facility in the country. The primary target audience of the educational activities is children and young adults because, as one GIFAP representative explained, "Changing adult habits is more difficult than developing good habits in children" (personal interview, Miguel Bermudez, Regional Representative, GIFAP, Jan. 17, 1992). Educational materials and courses are being developed for use in primary schools, rural secondary schools, vocational and agricultural schools, and the agricultural departments of the universities.

In addition, technical training is being developed for pesticide distributors to encourage them to promote safer use while they are selling their products. Ministry of Agriculture technicians are also targeted and are intended to be carriers of the safe-use message to small farmers throughout the country. Social security workers will be trained in an effort to use that system to educate rural housewives about pesticide hazards in the home as well as in their families' workplaces. Courses in the diagnosis and treatment of pesticide illnesses are also being developed for Guatemalan physicians, along with efforts to distribute atropine, the most common antidote for pesticide poisoning, to local health clinics.

Once the pilot project has been implemented and tested over three years, GIFAP plans to expand it into eight additional countries in Central and South America and the Caribbean. GIFAP reportedly will provide an additional $400,000 annually for this expansion and anticipates complementary funding from USAID's ROCAP.

By the end of 1991, ROCAP had unveiled its own ambitious safe-use strategy for Central America. Although broader in scope than the GIFAP program, it too relied predominantly on education and training in the proper techniques for using pesticides as a vehicle for overcoming the range of pesticide problems in the region.

ROCAP's Pesticide Management Activity (PMA) is a three-year, $4 million project composed of five separate areas, which in turn are part of the larger Regional Environmental and Natural Resource Management project, a ten-year, $30 million environmental program in Central America and the Caribbean (personal interview, Rick Clark, Jan. 15, 1992). Three of the five PMA components focus on training. The first relies on Peace Corps volunteers, to be trained in Costa Rica, who will promote safe use in rural communities throughout the region. The second component involves training by the Panamerican Agricultural School in Zamorano, Honduras, but focuses on agricultural technicians and, to a lesser degree, rural women, who will become messengers of the techniques among small farmers. The Zamorano training will be based on a five-day course using a popular education manual produced by GIFAP and approved by the EPA. The third component, conducted by the Instituto de Nutrición en Centro America y Panama, will train physicians in the region in diagnosis and treatment of pesticide-related illness through a correspondence course.

Another component of the program focuses on a data base on pests and pesticides in the region, to be developed in collaboration with the EPA and FDA. The final component will produce educational materials such as posters and manuals promoting the safe use of pesticides. These materials will be produced by GIFAP and funded in part by NACA as part of a close collaboration between the chemical industry and USAID (personal interview, Anarco Garcia, Jan. 17, 1992).

While the ROCAP strategy is intended to improve pesticide practices among campesinos, the PMA will concentrate on producers in nontraditional agriculture. As one ROCAP technician explained, ROCAP considers the new nontraditional sector the best avenue for diffusion of the safe-use message to campesinos in the region (personal interview, Rick Clark, ROCAP, Jan. 15, 1992). Presumably this assumption is based on the historical process of dissemination of pesticide technology from the traditional export crops like cotton into the basic grains sector based largely on campesinos, a process described in Chapter 2 and sometimes called the "algodonización de los granos basicos."

The other major international agency promoting safe use in Central America is the FAO. The FAO maintained its involvement in the pesticide issue throughout the 1970s and 1980s, both through its IPM efforts and through a range of seminars, conferences, and technical assistance programs. Then in 1991, the agency proposed a regionwide program focused on the code of conduct.

The FAO Central America program, like the GIFAP and USAID projects, is ambitious and multifaceted. The FAO has submitted a proposal for an estimated $2 million to the government of Holland to fund an initial three-year program to "rationalize the use of pesticides" by strengthening the capacity of Central American governments to implement the FAO Code of Conduct (personal interview, Genoveva Braun, FAO Central America Representative, Jan. 16, 1992). Sources close to the project indicate it will likely begin during 1994. The FAO will concentrate its efforts on a series of seminars in each country, combined with the provision of ongoing technical assistance, to strengthen pesticide legislation in each country, improve national pesticide registration systems, provide a data bank on pests and pesticides, improve laboratory services, and provide better technician training on the safe or rational use of pesticides.

An additional activity during this first phase involves an assessment of the resources available and additional resources required to implement a regional IPM program. This assessment will be the basis for a four-year second phase to the FAO program to promote IPM throughout the region. Assuming funding is available, it will begin no earlier than 1996.

The Limits of the Safe-Use Paradigm

The array of new efforts to resolve the pesticide problems in Central America are certainly a welcome, although long overdue, turn of events. The combination of projects may well reduce the continuing high rate of pesticide-related illnesses, environmental contamination, and ecologically based production problems. But some of the assumptions about the efficacy of safe use suggest that while there may be benefits, it will likely fall far short of a resolution of the problem.

Training and education in proper health and safety measures associated with pesticide hazards has clearly been lacking over the decades. Studies from both the cotton era (ICAITI 1977) (Cole et al. 1988) and the more recent rise of nontraditional exports (Conroy et al. forthcoming; Hoppin 1991) have demonstrated that pesticide users are woefully uninformed of hazards and fail to use proper protective measures. Consequently, the projects proposed by GIFAP, USAID, FAO, and others appear to be targeting a major source of the problem. Yet the scope of the problem is far beyond the most optimistic reach of these education and training efforts. GIFAP, for example, estimates that 1.9 million Guatemalans are in direct contact with pesticides. Not all are pesticide applicators, but one can assume that a large portion of this group needs some understanding of the hazards they face. Although the GIFAP program includes radio and other media efforts, along with training of technicians and other messengers of safe use, one must question if GIFAP's and other organizations' efforts combined can reach more than a small portion of this population.

In addition, as any educator will readily acknowledge, presenting a message and having that message understood and accepted are considerably different endeavors. One must assume that a change in behavior will require repeated and varying educational campaigns over an extended period, particularly in light of the decades already past during which farmers have received promotional messages urging them to use an ever greater volume and variety of chemicals, without reference to the hazards.

One example of the obstacles to training pesticide users suggests some reasons training and education may not resolve the problem. In the CARE Nicaragua program during the mid-1980s, workers received training in the mixing and loading of pesticides into airplanes for application on the cotton fields. They learned to use closed-system mixing and loading equipment, as well as basic health and safety procedures. A follow-up study found that only 5 percent of the workers trained just before the cotton season began were still on the job by mid-season (McConnell et al. 1992). The temporary, day-to-day nature of farm labor and the migratory structure of the agricultural labor market meant there was a constant turnover of personnel on the large farms where a significant portion of the farm laborers exposed to pesticides were employed. Unless training is conducted almost daily, an obvious impossibility, it is unlikely that many of the laborers exposed to pesticides at any given time will have been trained, particularly in the hazards they might encounter in their current work environment.

Providing adequate or even minimal training to the majority of the exposed population in Central America is almost impossible, which makes the GIFAP strategy of working through the educational institutions seem like a wise choice. If one can't reach the majority of the current pesticide users, this strategy at least promises to improve pesticide practices among future generations. One study in Costa Rica suggested that the vocational and agricultural schools were not only viable centers for educating future pesticide users, as GIFAP argued, but also were sites of serious pesticide hazards as students regularly used a range of highly toxic chemicals, at times leading to the poisoning of the young future farmers and agricultural technicians (Murray and McConnell 1987).

A recent evaluation of a teacher's guide on the relationship between environment, farming, and pesticides (a collaboration of chemical companies, government officials, and USAID in Costa Rica) also raised serious questions about the educational message being provided to Central American school children (Roldan 1991). The evaluation, conducted by the National University of Costa Rica, focused on the content of the pesticide unit of the curriculum. The assessment concluded that the basic message of the educational effort "created an image of dependence on pesticides by all types of producers. . . . the book is pro-pesticides, [and] does not give options for alternative attitudes, which invalidates the guide's claim to provide youth with more awareness of environmental reality" (Roldan 1991:3). The researchers found no discussion of alternative pest control strategies and observed that the educational effort appeared to be directed at raising awareness of the benefits of pesticides as much as the hazards. Although such a message is clearly consistent with the role and vision of the pesticide industry, it is questionable whether such a program belongs in the public schools. It is also questionable whether U.S. development agencies should be supporting the message, which is essentially, "Use pesticides safely, but by all means use pesticides." It is doubtful that such a message will ultimately contribute to a reduction in the pesticide problem.

Other problems with the safe-use message are more widespread and suggest possibly more-fundamental obstacles to the resolution of the pesticide problem. Much of the training of pesticide users focuses on the proper procedures for selecting, mixing, and applying pesticides, along with the appropriate personal protective measures and hygiene practices. The assumption is that once trained, workers will take greater precautions, such as relying on personal protective equipment and hygiene practices to reduce pesticide hazards.

There is ample evidence that for a variety of reasons, pesticide users generally ignore safe-use practices. In one USAID-funded study, participants in a workshop in Guatemala were surveyed about their use of personal protective equipment (CICP 1988 : 53). Only 1 out of 26 farmers reported using more than boots and a hat when applying pesticides. Another survey of Guatemalan farmers of nontraditional exports found that 89 percent did not use gloves when applying pesticides, 87 percent did not use glasses, and 42 percent relied on a handkerchief over the face for respiratory protection when spraying chemicals (Hoppin 1989 : 39). A regional survey found the use of personal protective equipment to vary among countries but to be consistently low for virtually all safety measures (Conroy et al. forthcoming) (Table 7-1).

Where training in the use of safety measures has been carried out, it

Table 7-1 Reported Use of Personal Protective Equipment Regionwide

Equipment	No response	No	Yes
Gloves	31 (16.15)	123 (64.06)	38 (19.79)
Boots	30 (15.62)	119 (61.98)	43 (22.40)
Overalls	39 (20.31)	139 (72.40)	14 (7.29)
Longsleeve shirt	29 (15.10)	123 (64.06)	40 (20.83)
Hat	38 (19.79)	116 (60.42)	38 (19.79)
Respirator	50 (26.04)	106 (55.21)	36 (18.75)
Other	39 (20.31)	144 (75.00)	9 (4.69)

SOURCE: Conroy et al. forthcoming.

[a] Report total was 192.

appears that improvements in personal protection have occurred, although the degree of change leaves some question as to whether it will actually reduce pesticide hazards and problems. The following excerpt from one USAID-funded study of pesticide use in the Guatemalan highlands is enlightening on this question:

> Those who stated that they had received a full and careful explanation from the pesticide vendors consistently reported taking more precautions in applying pesticide. In some cases, the difference between those who had received a good explanation and those who had not is significant. The following percentages of respondents reporting on use of various equipment items came from the good-explanation group: overalls when spraying, 55.1%, masks, 59.5%, gloves, 63.2% and 66.7% always used eyeglasses. . . .
>
> Of those who stated that they always took a bath after pesticide use, 51.3% came from the well-informed group. Of those who said they changed their clothes after spraying, 50.0% came from this group, while 46.8% of those who stated they washed their faces after pesticide application also came from the group that had received the more complete explanation of the dangers of incorrect pesticide use. . . . Careful instructions . . . may play an important role in improving the safety precautions used by farmers. (CICP 1988 : 59–60)

Indeed there may have been improvements in personal protection, but with only 46 to 66 percent adopting safety precautions after careful instructions, one must question what it will take to assure the safety of the large minority, and in some instances the majority, of trained workers who continue to use pesticides in hazardous ways.

It has often been asked, if workers have been informed about pesticide hazards, why do they continue to work in ways that are likely to expose them to hazards? The answers to that question are complex and not necessarily adequate. One common explanation is that personal protective equipment is uncomfortable to use, unaffordable, or otherwise unavailable. That certainly would explain a portion of the problem. Another explanation, more popular among farm managers who employ laborers, is that no matter how much training one provides, some workers are just more careless than others. Like the previous explanation, in some instances this may be the case, but it could just as easily be a case of blaming the victim.[2]

Yet there are more powerful reasons why many workers fail to respond to the message of safe use, reasons that belie the optimism accompanying the training and education strategy. A recent case of mass worker poisoning in Honduras demonstrates the social reality in which pesticides are normally used and suggests why pesticide problems will likely persist in spite of the best-intentioned efforts at training and education. In the spring of 1989, a group of fifteen workers, mostly teenage women ranging in age from thirteen to eighteen, were poisoned while applying carbofuran, a carbamate, to the melon fields of Choluteca (Murray 1991). According to the government investigator of the incident, the workers had been applying the pesticide with their bare hands, sprinkling the granulated or powdered chemical throughout the field. They stopped to eat lunch without washing their hands, thereby ingesting the chemical residues with their food. Within a short time they became severely ill.

The most basic pesticide safety training would have addressed the main causes of this poisoning incident. Workers would have been instructed to use personal protective equipment, in this case rubber gloves, which would have avoided the primary source of dermal contact with the chemical. Instructions would necessarily have included the need to wash one's hands before eating lunch, further reducing the likelihood of ingestion of pesticide residues. But the instructions in safety procedures would have been useless if the minimal infrastructure, such as safety equipment and wash facilities, was absent. In many if not most instances, those are exactly the work conditions found in the developing world. In the Cholutecan case, the melon workers were not provided gloves or other safety equipment by their employer. Workers did not have adequate water available for washing, nor was soap provided. More important, workers normally had only twenty minutes for their lunch break before returning to apply pesticides, hardly enough time to walk the considerable distance necessary to find a place to wash one's hands and eat before having to return to work.

This example was not an isolated case. Poisonings in Nicaragua reached epidemic proportions in the late 1980s because of the use of the same pesticide in the same manner (McConnell 1988).[3] These cases demonstrate how the effects of training and access to personal protective equipment, as touted by the proponents of the safe-use strategy, are mediated by the social relations in the workplace and the general lack of commitment by employers to improving worker protection.

Yet another shortcoming makes it difficult to overcome the hazards posed by pesticides. Various studies have demonstrated that even when used as instructed, personal protective equipment does not provide adequate and consistent protection. This is partly because people rely on the wrong kinds of personal protection. Swayed by the noxious smell of some pesticides, many people tend to believe that poisoning is most often the result of pesticide inhalation. So respirators, or frequently handkerchiefs, which offer almost no respiratory protection, are the pro-

tective measure of choice. Respirators were the most frequently used
piece of personal protective equipment identified by cotton workers in
one survey, with 38 percent reportedly relying on this form of protection
(Cole et al. 1988:126). Long-sleeved shirts were used by 28 percent of
the respondents, rubber boots by 20 percent, hats by 18 percent, and
overalls by 17 percent.[4]

One consequence of this bias in favor of respiratory protection was
found in Nicaragua in the late 1980s when farm workers successfully
pressured the government to purchase more protective equipment for
workers on the state cotton farms (Murray 1989b). The Nicaraguan
Ministry of Agriculture subsequently purchased thousands of respirators. Since respirators were manufactured outside Nicaragua, the purchase represented a substantial commitment of scarce foreign currency
to worker safety (McConnell 1988). It also reflected the common igno-
rance and biases concerning the nature of pesticide hazards. The vast
majority of worker poisonings in cotton farming did not come from inhalation but from dermal absorption of chemicals. Dermal contact was
identified as the route of exposure in 68 percent of the poisonings reported by Nicaraguan doctors (Cole et al. 1988:125), suggesting that
respirators would have provided little protection in the majority of
cases. Other studies have shown that respirators, even where appropriate, frequently are not fitted or maintained well enough to protect the
user adequately.

Appropriate protection in the majority of cases involves either adequate coverage of the skin or hygiene measures such as bathing and
washing of hands. Such protection does not involve significant expenditures of foreign currency, since adequate dermal protection in most
instances could be provided by cotton overalls or long-sleeved shirts,
which can be produced throughout the region from local materials. All
the countries in Central America can also produce rubber boots and
gloves at a relatively low cost as well. Simple skin protection, when
combined with regular hygiene practices, could significantly reduce the
hazards of dermal exposure.

The safe-use strategy is further limited by the continued belief that
government institutions in the region can regulate pesticide use. This
is the essential assumption of the FAO Code of Conduct and the project
the FAO has proposed for Central America. To assume that the governments can adopt stricter legislation and then implement it rigorously
ignores the history of weak states in the region and of regulatory efforts
that have been blocked or compromised by interests with little or no
commitment to the safe use of pesticides.

More important, this emphasis on the public sector ignores the influence of the structural adjustment policies of the World Bank/IMF,

which in most cases have reduced Central American government institutions to inconsequential agencies with limited capacities. For example, the Secretaría de Recursos Naturales of Honduras, the agency charged with implementing both agricultural and environmental policy, saw its operating budget reduced by 50 percent during the 1980s (USAID 1990). It is unlikely that this agency can significantly expand its control of pesticide use when it lacks sufficient funding for such basic necessities as salaries for field personnel and vehicle maintenance. Similarly, a U.S. Government Accounting Office study of regulatory programs in five Latin American countries concluded that most were woefully ineffective (Harman 1990).

In the absence of a major infusion of funding and resources into the public sectors of these countries it is doubtful that the FAO project will go far toward resolving the pesticide problem. As one recent analysis of the code of conduct concluded, "Much of the Code, in fact, describes a fantasy world, in which capable regulatory agents from competent, noncorrupt Third World governments are constantly in the countryside, enjoying the voluntary support and cooperation of private industry, making sure that naturally prudent and self-reliant individual farm workers will have all the information they need to avoid risks of chemical exposure" (Paarlberg 1991 : 23).

The FAO effort may indeed contribute to a greater appreciation of the need to control pesticide hazards in the region, but it seems doubtful that this project, or the other safe-use projects, will fundamentally alter the pattern of pesticide problems. In fact the current array of projects leaves the impression that a cornucopia of resources is being devoted to a strategy that is likely to have only limited benefits. In addition, the major role played by the pesticide industry in the safe-use paradigm appears to compromise some of the benefits such a strategy might provide. The message "use safely, but in any case use" pesticides, likely will undermine the ability to engage alternative nonchemical or low-chemical strategies against pesticide problems. Although the industry claims to be promoting the use of the minimum amount of pesticides necessary, pesticide salespeople continue to be paid largely through sales commissions, receiving greater remuneration for greater pesticide sales, a practice more likely to maximize pesticide marketing rather than minimize pesticide use.

Conclusion

As noted earlier, safe-use strategies are, in principle, important contributions to the resolution of pesticide-related problems. Various activities under way or proposed by the chemical industry, USAID, the

FAO, and others will undoubtedly benefit some of the people at risk of experiencing pesticide-related health or other problems. But in the rush to implement new projects, the efforts to resolve pesticide problems by developing alternative strategies for pest control may have been weakened. This abundance of safe-use efforts may be wasteful of scarce resources, and, more important, it may obscure or undermine efforts for fundamental change. By consuming the limited amount of funding available for addressing pesticide problems, and by providing a false sense that the problem is being adequately addressed, safe use may actually be perpetuating the problem by dominating the discourse on pesticide issues.

In addition, although the efforts of GIFAP may be laudable, they must also be recognized as pre-emptive. It is hard to imagine the pesticide industry doing otherwise, since the promotion of real alternatives implies a potentially significant decline in the fortunes of the chemical sector. If competing strategies can focus on farmer-first methods, which generate locally developed and controlled technologies, the chemical industry may find itself marginalized as new techniques come to depend on methods not easily commodified, patented, or marketed by transnational corporations. The promotion of safe use thus addresses a series of pesticide-related problems while helping to sustain a powerful set of economic interests.

The real potential for change in the competition between the safe-use and alternative paradigms lies not with the pesticide industry but with the local and international development institutions. As the problems become increasingly apparent, the efforts for their resolution may become increasingly significant. The evolution from safe use to alternative agriculture in the CARE program, for example, suggests that NGOs may provide considerable impetus for more fundamental resolutions to the pesticide problems in the region.

Although USAID, FAO, and others may be more resistant to change, there is still some room for hope. For example, the recent Twenty-sixth Biennial Conference of the FAO, held in Rome November 11 to 28, 1991, adopted several improvements in the code of conduct, plus a series of recommendations to pursue sustainable agriculture based on reducing chemical and other inputs and seeking more stable production systems oriented to the long term (FAO 1992). On the other hand, resistance to change remains strong within the agency, as the FAO's reaffirmation of its faith in agrochemical technology, expressed in the FAO 2000 report, demonstrates (Dinham 1991).

As long as the safe-use paradigm dominates the discourse on pesticide problems and their resolutions, progress will be slow. One can only hope that the increasing attention to pesticide problems will eventually weaken the dominance of this paradigm and lead to a reorienting of problem-solving strategies. Until that time, the Third World will likely repeat the pattern of development, crisis, and inequitable social change that has characterized its agricultural sector throughout the postwar period of chemical-intensive farming.

8

Pesticides, Development, and Crisis: Toward a Resolution

I n little more than a decade after the end of the Second World War,
pesticides had become a central technology in the modernization
of Third World agriculture. Without the control of the boll weevil
and the anopheles mosquito provided by organochlorine and organophosphate compounds, the cotton boom in Central America and elsewhere would not have been possible. By overcoming those barriers, the
technology became a key to the generation of many great fortunes in
the developing world and a cornerstone of the economic and social system constructed on the foundation of agroexports.

Yet within a very short time after the takeoff of chemical-intensive
agriculture, the technology became the source of ecological, economic,
and social problems. In some instances these problems came to rival or
surpass many of the gains the technology had fostered. Economic fortunes were lost even faster than they were made as resistant and resur-
gent pests wiped out entire harvests. Social discontent and unrest followed in the wake of both the success and the subsequent failure of
agricultural development, as the problems of pesticide dependence combined with broader social and economic problems to bring the cotton
sector to a virtual standstill. By the 1980s, the once booming cotton
economy had become a pale shadow of its Golden Age two decades
earlier.

As if the tragedy of the cotton era were not enough, it was re-created
(perhaps as farce) in the 1980s through the development of nontraditional exports, as various countries throughout the Caribbean Basin
experienced renewed pesticide crises in an accelerated, although more
localized replication of the cotton era. It appears that development planners have embraced the Faustian bargain inherent in agrochemical technology, trading long-term (although increasingly shorter-term) crisis for
more immediate gain.

Even more disconcerting is the dearth (in spite of several decades of
experience with these boom and bust cycles of development) of alternatives actually being employed on a large scale in the agricultural
sectors of developing countries.[1] Only within the last few years have
concerted efforts been made to alter this historic pattern in Central
American export agriculture. It remains questionable whether even
these efforts represent a genuine alternative or are more an attempt to
tinker with the most glaring weaknesses of the existing development
paradigm, while sustaining chemical-intensive farming a while longer.

Why, in the face of over four decades of persistent and glaring problems, has this technology continued to dominate agricultural development?

The Persistence of Pesticide-Dependent Development

The development process has been surprisingly consistent since the end of World War II. After the war, with U.S. production capacity at an all-time high, stimulating growth in the periphery became a significant concern for U.S. economic and development planners. The task became one of modernizing productive sectors in the developing world to make them more attractive for investment and development ventures, which in turn would assure their continued growth as commodity suppliers and consumer markets. Capital-intensive development and production systems became the order of the day and have remained the primary vehicle for Third World development ever since.

Development assistance focused on restructuring Third World economies in a manner that integrated them into the global economy. Financial assistance went to improving productive enterprises and to developing the infrastructure necessary for profitable investment ventures. Roads and ports were built to facilitate the movement of goods and services. Industrial components such as pesticide manufacturing and formulating plants, cotton gins, and beef processing plants were financed to stimulate Third World export production as well as the consumption of First World inputs. In the process, Third World economies became inextricably linked to the accelerating cycles of capital-intensive production, consumption, and reinvestment that came to characterize the global economy (Aglietta 1979; de Janvry 1981).

In agriculture, this meant increasing productivity and crop yields through the introduction and promotion of high technology consistent with the Green Revolution. Relying on various technological innovations, development planners sought to integrate Third World agriculture into a postwar period of global economic expansion. Pesticides and other technologies were imported from the developed world to accelerate the extraction of profits. Short-term, growth-stimulating development was emphasized in regions like Central America and the Caribbean (Guerra-Borges 1989).

Pesticides provided greater control of some of the primary ecological obstacles to intensifying agricultural production. Crops could be grown in a monocultural and repetitive manner, allowing a more intensive use of the land. Some chemicals, particularly herbicides, allowed significant reductions in labor costs and further cut agricultural production time, during which capital investment was tied up. Pesticides were an important part of this development process, not only because they generated wealth by improving profits in agricultural production but also because the technology, as a key input, was a highly profitable commodity in its own right in the agricultural production process.

In addition, the development process in Central America strengthened the socioeconomic structure that had historically characterized the region, in what has been described as "additive development" (Gorostiaga and Marchetti 1988). Land and capital were already highly concentrated before the postwar development boom, but the capital-intensive development schemes that emerged from this period increased their concentration even more. With the introduction of pesticides, agricultural interests could exploit economies of scale biased in favor of larger and transnational operations, further concentrating land and displacing peasants and smaller producers (Williams 1986; Conroy et al. forthcoming). Thus pesticides actually heightened the already acute inequity between rich and poor in Latin America.

Pesticides, insofar as they sustained the development of new crops like cotton, broadened the elite strata in some societies. Urban investors from San Salvador, Guatemala City, and Managua joined the traditional landed aristocracy in pursuing the agricultural bonanza of the cotton boom (Colburn 1986; Enriquez 1991), but they did not alter the historical pattern of severe inequity and antidemocratic rule in the region. The new elites merely joined the existing aristocracy in the exploitation of land and labor. The pesticide technology served to support the historical pattern of Third World socioeconomic development.

Similarly, the promotion of nontraditional exports during the 1980s was intended to mediate the dominance of the traditional landed elites in the region (Barham et al. 1992). But the new development strategy only reinforced many of the social, economic, and ecological problems. Pesticides were again not only an integral part of the development process but also an integral part of the problems this process generated. In addition, the nontraditionals helped integrate these local economies with the global economy, but unlike the cotton interests, the dominant actors in the nontraditional sector have been able to move relatively freely as pesticide and other problems emerge. Where pesticide-induced crises bankrupted many cotton producers, the biggest operators in the nontraditional crops have learned to anticipate such crises. Increasingly, large-scale operations simply move to new locations to escape pesticide problems. In so doing, they also relieve the pressures to find solutions to the crisis-generating effects of the technology. In the wake of such moves entrepreneurs often find new investment opportunities in the form of cheapened land values and impoverished labor forces. In effect, the transnationals have restructured their operations to make better use of the global system and to enhance their exploitation of local settings.[2]

Institutionalizing Pesticide-Dependent Development

The array of institutional forces that developed during this period supported the persistence of chemical-intensive farming. Institutions arose both internationally and nationally, within the public as well as the private sectors, and became dependent upon the perpetuation of pesticide use.

Internationally, the FAO, the World Bank, and USAID became advocates of the high-technology, growth-stimulating strategy. In an effort to generate quick growth, new investment capital, and attractive investment opportunities, these agencies promoted pesticides as a central part of policies to maximize yield and productivity. Pesticide-dependent farming became such a common part of development institutions' assistance programs that private and public institutions often appeared to operate in unison when promoting the technology. Pesticide industry representatives sat on many government commissions and exchanged places regularly with government policymakers through a revolving door of government and private-sector employment. This arrangement continues today in the nontraditional agricultural development process as managers of transnational agricultural and chemical companies move into management roles in USAID projects, and USAID officials have assumed public and private-sector positions related to nontraditional agriculture (Conroy et al. forthcoming).

Pesticide use was also encouraged by the governments of the developing countries. The historical linkage between the executive branch and the landed aristocracies in Central America and elsewhere meant that pesticide-dependent monocultural production, as well as the fortunes of those interests linked to the local chemical industry, was well supported by government services. Consider, for example, the discussion in Chapter 2 of the banking and financial groups involved in the Central American cotton boom. These groups included such ruling families as the Somozas of Nicaragua and the Christianis of El Salvador. Third World governments became particularly adept at keeping the costs of the pesticide problems external to the balance sheets of the large-scale operations that relied on the technology. Large landowners were rarely, if ever, held accountable for the environmental degradation, public health problems, or other negative effects of their heavy use of pesticides. Further, the policies of financial institutions encouraged more intensive exploitation of land and resources, heightening the heavy dependence on and the destructive effects of the pesticide technology.

The promise of short-term growth inherent in chemical-intensive agriculture was appealing to Third World regimes in part because it held out hope of relief for the impoverished rural sectors in these countries, which in turn held out promise of relief from the social unrest and political instability that plagued Third World governments. But once on the path of chemical-intensive agriculture, these regimes frequently found it easier to deny or ignore the pesticide problem when the technology contributed more to turmoil than prosperity, instead of seeking changes in agricultural practices, particularly when the alternative was a confrontation with a formidable alliance of local and international interests linked to the continued reliance on pesticides.

Various departments of the government ministries became dependent upon chemical-intensive agriculture. For example, the plant protection divisions of the ministries of agriculture became important centers of pesticide promotion. Once farming was organized around short-term agricultural production schemes, plant protection officials were faced with the continual task of improving upon and fine tuning the existing farming systems. This most commonly took the form of promoting new pesticides to replace older ones. Innovation essentially became input substitution.

Public educational institutions perpetuated the dependence on the chemical paradigm. Pesticide-based agricultural research dominated international and Third World research institutions for several decades in the postwar era. During this period most of the policymakers, agricultural technicians, and extensionists still working in these regions were trained in pesticide-dependent farming. Thus the technical resource-base upon which planning and policy were built became indoctrinated in the benefits and necessity of pesticide technology.

In the private sector, the chemical industry was the key force behind the continued emphasis on pesticides in Third World agriculture. Through the influence of individual companies in both the developed and developing world, and through the combined influence of the industry lobbying organizations such as GIFAP and NACA, policies promoting pesticides continued to be adopted by international and national government entities long after the negative effects of pesticides had become widely known. With the increasing integration between agricultural production, food processing, transportation, and food marketing that characterized transnational agribusiness firms, pesticides remained a logical part of transnational business.

Individual Self-interest and
Pesticide-Dependent Development

The persistence of chemical-intensive farming was also the product of an array of individuals and groups who saw their own interests tied to the continued reliance on pesticides. The most obvious examples were those individuals involved in the marketing of pesticides. The highly developed system of pesticide sales and distribution in Central America and the Caribbean included thousands of individuals, from company executives to local merchants, whose livelihoods depended on the sale of pesticides. For example, as noted previously, most pesticide sales representatives were paid on a commission basis, which rewarded those who can sell ever-greater quantities of their company's products. Thus the pressures from the pesticide companies to continue to increase sales in the region became internalized through the career aspirations of the company agents, who promoted increased pesticide use among the region's farmers.

But less obvious was the link between the technology and the interests of the agricultural technicians and policymakers. Trained in the chemical-intensive methods of modern farming, field technicians often resisted new and innovative reforms that called for the reduction or elimination of the technology. The alternative strategies depended upon ever greater levels of training and more precise understandings of complex ecological systems. This training was difficult to obtain, and the lack of it posed threats to the jobs and even the organizational systems of agricultural production upon which these technicians had built their careers.

Development specialists similarly had built careers on the promotion of the Green Revolution and were deeply committed to the wisdom of high-yielding, short-term, growth-oriented farming systems. Pesticides had always been an integral part of these systems, and development planners frequently saw challenges to chemical-intensive farming (often rightly so) as attempts to undercut the very systems to which these specialists had dedicated their careers and upon which they saw their future interests riding.

Political figures in Third World governments were generally committed to maintaining the status quo as part of the realpolitik of governing. Challenges to chemical-intensive agriculture were frequently seen as part of greater plots to unsettle the political order and thus were resisted and discredited, along with a wide range of other demands. One example was the reaction in 1987 of Costa Rica's minister of health, Edgar Mohs, who wrote an editorial in the country's leading newspaper at a time when various groups and individuals were pressuring the administration of president Oscar Arias for reform of the government's pesticide policies. Mohs warned that subversive elements in his country, which he linked with an international communist movement, had realized they could not generate opposition and revolutionary ferment through traditional means, and consequently "they appear interested in propagandizing about liquor and cigarettes, pesticides, mother's milk, child nutrition and the hazards of medicines" (Mohs 1986).

The resistance against challenges to chemical-intensive agriculture was nurtured by the personal and professional linkages between officials of the executive branch of government and the pesticide industry and agribusiness representatives. Similar to elite networks in the First World (Domhoff 1978), Third World government and business leaders often had close family ties, were educated at the same schools (frequently in the United States), and belonged to the same social and professional organizations. The continual promotion of pesticide-based agriculture was carried out through these informal channels, in addition to more visible and formal avenues of influence.

A Countervailing Tendency to
Pesticide-Dependent Development

The consequences of this amalgam of interests and forces perpetuating the heavy use of pesticides have been significant for small producers and the rural labor force, and in some instances for entire sectors of Third World agricultural export economies. Pesticide-driven development has left in its wake a great many losers, both in the "high stakes gamble of nontraditional agriculture" (Conroy et al. forthcoming), and in the preceding cotton era. These included not only bankrupt and displaced farmers and increasingly marginalized rural laborers but also the many victims of pesticide poisoning and a rural populace forced to live in degraded environmental conditions.

But such impoverishment and degradation have not gone unchallenged. The very success in perpetuating chemical-intensive agriculture has fostered pressures for change, in pesticide-dependent farming and in the development process in which it has flourished. In some instances the pressures for fundamental changes in the direction of Third World development have only been implicit in the quests for relief from the pesticide problem. In others the pressure has been far more explicit. Combined, these various pressures suggest that the recurring and ongoing nature of pesticide problems has contributed to a larger countervailing tendency for the pursuit of an alternative path of agricultural development.

The modern history of agricultural development in Central America and the Caribbean is replete with examples of victims of the pesticide technology pressing for changes to chemical-intensive agricultural development. Farm worker unions, peasant associations, and local environmental groups in various parts of Latin America have made pesticide problems an issue of organizational concern, as well as a focus of contention in their dealings with governments and other institutions. The example of the Nicaraguan farm workers in León, who confronted President Daniel Ortega and a group of government officials in a community meeting in 1987 to demand greater protective measures and health services for workers handling or exposed to pesticides, is illustrative (Murray 1989). The organized pressure from the rural workers led to a flurry of government actions intended to relieve some of the immediate sources of discontent. In so doing, the Sandinista government may have helped push pesticide problems high on the farm worker agenda for the future.

Examples of popular and grassroots pressures for change abound in Central America. Just before the recent peace accords in El Salvador, a large federation of cooperatives began circulating a proposal for a new cooperative program called Tierra Viva, Living Earth (NEST 1992). The vision presented by the Salvadoran cooperativists encompassed an array of fundamental issues suggesting that the efforts to resolve the pesticide problem in Central American agriculture were becoming a constituent element of a much greater quest for an alternative course of development. The organization proposed developing a pesticide-free farming system, including farmer-initiated experimentation for alternative technology development, as well as the development of organic nontraditional export crops combined with the production of organically grown traditional subsistence crops like corn and beans. The organization's plan also proposed a highly democratic and participatory system for decision-making, training, and technology development, as well as a system for the equitable distribution of the benefits of these strategies.

Similarly, several broad-based coalitions of farmers in Costa Rica have become increasingly militant in challenging current agricultural development policies in that country, including demonstrations in the capital city and blockages of major highways (Vunderink 1989; Stonich et al. 1992). Pesticide problems have been among the issues of contention raised by these groups. The alternatives they have presented are explicitly focused on the creation of more sustainable, ecologically rational, and socially just opportunities for small and medium-size farmers (CNPMPJD 1991).

The institutional base for the opposition to pesticide-dependent development has been greatly strengthened by the emergence of hundreds of local and internationally based nongovernmental organizations (Sanford et al. 1989; Annis 1992). These groups have tended to work closely with farmers and farm workers at a local level, developing responses to pesticide problems and providing technical, organizational, and financial resources in the pursuit of alternative development strategies. International nongovernmental organizations like CARE, the American Friends Service Committee, OXFAM, and Catholic Relief Services have focused explicitly on pesticide-related health and production problems in Central America (Murray 1989). In addition, national nongovernmental organizations like the Programa de Plaguicidas, Desarrollo, Salud y Ambiente at the Universidad Nacional in Costa Rica, have worked as advocates for pesticide policy changes and for alternative farming projects throughout the Central American region (DANIDA 1992).

The Pesticide Action Network (PAN) has also become an important force in the international policy arena and has effectively challenged the proponents of chemical-intensive agriculture on a number of occasions (Paarlberg 1991). Moreover, PAN has become increasingly important as a technical support organization for local Third World organizations in identifying key pesticide problems and in developing strategies for their resolution. Newly formed regional offices of PAN have appeared in Mexico, the Dominican Republic, and Colombia. A network of local alternative agriculture organizations has also recently developed throughout Latin America to provide a means for exchanging technical and policy information on nonchemical farming systems (Altieri and Yurjevic 1989).

Other organizations like the Movimiento Ambiental de Nicaragua and the International Union for the Conservation of Nature in Costa Rica have made the pesticide issue a part of a broader environmental program. These environmental organizations have generally identified pesticides as one of the primary issues for galvanizing popular support for a broader environmental agenda. Local environmental organizations have been strengthened through their linkages to international organizations like Greenpeace or through access to First World funding sources, particularly the development programs of Nordic governments.[3]

There are also a variety of government institutions in Central America and the Caribbean that have begun to provide a weak but nevertheless important institutional base for the pursuit of alternative development strategies. The ministries of agriculture remain the bastions of chemical-intensive agriculture, but groups responsible for various natural resource or environmental programs within these agencies have become more vocal about curbing governmental policies promoting pesticide-dependent production. For example, the personnel of IRENA, Nicaragua's Environmental Institute within the Ministry of Agriculture, have become some of the leading spokespersons on environmental issues in that country. In addition, representatives of the ministries of health in Nicaragua, Costa Rica, and Guatemala have spoken out both locally and in international fora against the public health problems caused by pesticides.

International institutions like the United Nations have also become an important institutional base for the challenge to chemical-intensive agriculture. The UNEP and WHO have for many years served as counterforces to the proponents of the chemical paradigm within the FAO (Paarlberg 1991). The influence of these agencies has been significantly less than that of the institutions associated with pesticide-dependent development, but they have provided critical opportunities for individuals and groups working within and outside the United Nations system to influence pesticide-related development policies.

Pesticides and Changes in the Global Economy

It has become increasingly clear that the resource base upon which development has been built is not unlimited.[4] It has also become apparent that the Green Revolution's high-technology farming strategies, as well as the more general faith in development that stimulates short-term growth, have not solved the glaring socioeconomic and ecological problems facing the majority of people in the world. These strategies are being recognized as central forces in the creation and exacerbation of these problems.

The search for resolutions to these problems, such as those associated with the pesticide technology, has led to a convergence of efforts to create alternative production systems and to pursue alternative economic strategies, which essentially represent the beginning of an alternative vision of development.

The existing market economy does not appear to be a viable structure for developing or disseminating such noncommodifiable technologies. Instead, cooperative systems and farmer organizations are developing their own technology experimentation and transfer systems. For example, organic coffee cooperatives have developed in recent years in Mexico and Central and South America. While still relying on export production, the organic coffee producers have become part of alternative marketing and distribution systems that seek to build closer links between Third World producers and First World consumers, promoting not only pesticide-free products but also alternative social and economic arrangements as well (Nigh 1991). More important, organic coffee is seen by these producers as a transition crop to more diversified production oriented to the local market, as cooperatives use their coffee income to finance experimentation and development in more diverse and

integrated systems for producing basic grains and other crops for local
and regional consumption.

Cooperatives from the Soconusco of southern Mexico, in the northern Nicaraguan departments of Chinandega and Estelí, and down
through the mountainous regions of Perú, have all begun to network
around questions of marketing and production. As these networks develop, the groups have begun sharing other ideas such as production
system innovations and even alternative forms of transnational social
and political organization. Counterposing social organization for advanced technology as a solution to social problems has become an integral component of an emerging alternative vision of development (Ekins 1992; Korten and Alfonso 1983; Freeman 1989).

Conclusion

An alternative vision of development, while still imminent in the
array of efforts being pursued, is more consistent with the ecological
imperatives of long-term sustainability, balance, and diversity and
stands in contrast to the socioeconomic dynamics of the current development process. For example, some alternative agricultural systems
that reduce or eliminate pesticides rely on smaller-scale landholding
patterns with greater crop diversity. These alternative farming strategies may provide support for the development of alternatives to the social structure of the traditional landed aristocracies of Central America
and the Caribbean.

The alternative technologies being developed for pest control are frequently not commodifiable and thus may contribute to the greater au-
tonomy and sustainability of systems more dependent on cooperation
than competition. These alternative technologies are frequently based
on traditional knowledge or the lessons learned from the failure of pesticides (Bentley 1989; Bentley and Andrews 1991). Both the development and the dissemination of these technologies may foster alternative
systems of communication and interaction, which in turn have implications for socioeconomic change.

Such implications are little more than speculation at present, but the
incipient tendencies toward an alternative course of development are
emerging. As one observer recently asked, "Are we not beginning to
inhabit a gap between the discursive practice of development and a new
one, which is slowly and painfully coming into existence, but which
will establish us as different from the previous bankrupt order, so that
we will not be obliged to speak the same truths, the same language, and
prescribe the same strategies?" (Escobar 1992).

The efforts to solve the pesticide problem are a relatively small but nevertheless significant part of an overall movement toward the creation of a more economically viable, socially just, and ecologically sound course of development. This fundamental shift in the nature of Third World development is unlikely to occur without the commitment and involvement of a wide range of interests and organizations, including those seeking a resolution to the pesticide problem. While it is too early to claim that either the resolution to the pesticide problem or the creation of an alternative course of development is at hand, it seems clear that it is in the linking of such projects that we are likely to find the best prospects for more viable and sustainable future societies.

Notes

CHAPTER 1: DEVELOPMENT'S UNKEPT PROMISE

1. Escobar (1988:3) defined the development discourse as "the systematic elaboration of fields of knowledge and institutions which made possible the establishment in the Third World of forms of power through which individuals, government officials and, sometimes, whole communities recognized themselves as 'underdeveloped,' as unfinished manifestations of an European ideal."

2. Throughout this book the term "pests" is used broadly, to include not only insects but also plant diseases, weeds, rodents, and other related sources of crop destruction and economic loss. Similarly, the term "pesticides" includes insecticides, herbicides, fungicides, nematocides, avicides, and other chemicals.

3. Throughout this book I will have occasion to discuss individual pesticides. I recognize that the wide variety of pesticides could be seen as a variety of technologies, but for the purposes of developing a deeper analysis of pesticide problems I will combine all pesticides under the general rubric of agrochemical technology.

CHAPTER 2: PESTICIDES AND THE CENTRAL AMERICAN COTTON BOOM

1. By 1991, pesticide use in cotton had fallen to only 11 percent of world consumption as pesticide use increased in other crops (Dinham 1991:15).

2. In the Cañete Valley of Peru, for example, other important cotton pests before World War II included the leafworm *Anomis texana* Riley, the aphid known as melaza (*Aphis gossypii* Glover), minor bollworm (*Mescinea peruella* Schauss), the white scale *Hemichionaspis minor* Mark., and the cotton stainer *Dysdercus peruvianus* Guerin. After 1939 the bollworm *Heliothis virescens* Fabricius also became an important cotton pest in the valley (Barducci 1972:427–428).

3. Probably the red locust, but the term has been used colloquially in Nicaragua and elsewhere to identify a variety of different pests.

4. See Repetto 1985 and Rosset 1987 for a discussion of various forms of pesticide-related subsidies in the developing world.

5. See Hansen 1990 for a review of the history of the World Bank's role in the dissemination of pesticide technology in the developing world.

6. OPIC was particularly active in aiding the proliferation of pesticides in the Third World. Between 1974 and 1976, three of the top four recipients of guarantees backed by U.S. taxpayers were U.S. chemical companies, with Dow receiving $181 million and W. R. Grace receiving $70 million (Weir and Shapiro 1981:51).

CHAPTER 3: COTTON AND THE PESTICIDE CRISIS

1. See Martorell and Kaplowitz 1990 and Martorell et al. 1991 for an analysis of undernutrition in the Guatemalan highlands.
2. The expansion of beef production in this period also played an important role in Central American agrarian change. See Stonich 1993.
3. See for example Brockett 1988, Bulmer-Thomas 1987, Williams 1986, Barry 1987, and Booth and Walker 1989.
4. See Faber 1993 and Leonard 1987. See also Zuvekas 1992 for a discussion of the lack of in-depth analysis of the ecological dimensions of the crisis.
5. This conceptual formulation appears in the work of Chapin and Wasserstrom 1983 and Faber 1993.
6. Central American cotton was increasingly picked by machine. For example, in 1975 there were only thirteen active mechanical harvesters in Nicaragua (Enriquez 1991:167), the most technologically advanced of the region's cotton-producing countries (ICAITI 1977). Ten years later there were two hundred mechanical harvesters, with 42 percent of the Nicaraguan cotton harvested by machine.
7. See Altieri and Yurjevic 1989 and Carroll et al. 1990 for discussions of agroecology.
8. See Chapter 6 for an analysis of alternative pest control measures pursued during this era.
9. The increase in estimated illnesses was both the result of a greater appreciation for the scope of the problem and also the result of an increase in the volume of pesticides used in the developing world. See WHO 1989. But even this latter estimate, according to WHO, was highly conservative and lacked even the minimally necessary documentation.
10. See Wright 1990 for a discussion of the public health impact of the shift from organochlorines to organophosphates in Mexican agriculture.
11. Parathion was also the source of the vast majority of farm worker poisonings in the United States during the same period (Hayes 1982:282–283).
12. One useful reference point for understanding the scope of underreporting is an article written by a California public health official during the same period, in which he estimated that California's system for recording pesticide illness, considered to be among the most thorough in the world, captured as little as 1 or 2 percent of the actual poisonings occurring in California (Kahn 1976).
13. See, for example, Riding 1980. See also Bull 1982.
14. See Murray 1989b for a more complete description of this program.
15. It is important to note that the department of León was going through considerable change during this period, with cotton production declining sig-

nificantly to be replaced primarily by corn. In 1984, two thirds of the cases reported through the public health system occurred in cotton farming (Cole 1988:125). By 1989 only 14 percent of the poisonings were attributed to cotton, while roughly half occurred in corn (Keifer and Pacheco 1991). The shift in crops probably reduced the overall volume and variety of pesticides used in the department, which in turn probably reduced pesticide poisoning per capita from what one might have expected when cotton was the dominant crop. This suggests that the overall illness estimates from León for 1989 still understated the scope of the problem during the earlier cotton boom years. On the other hand, pesticide use has increased in corn and has led to significant increases in poisonings in that sector (McConnell et al. 1990).

16. The debate over the carcinogenicity of organochlorines, and over the degree of long-term risk posed by pesticides, has continued for decades. See Epstein 1979 and *Agrichemical Age* 1989 for opposing views.

CHAPTER 4: ADDRESSING THE CRISIS THROUGH
NONTRADITIONAL AGRICULTURE

1. For a review of the various studies and policy proposals addressing the regional crisis, as well as a discussion of the continuing lack of concern for environmental issues within these works, see Zuvekas 1992.

2. "The more things change, the more they remain the same."

3. Original beneficiary countries, as of September 30, 1986, included Anguilla, Antigua and Barbuda, Aruba, Bahamas, Barbados, Belize, British Virgin Islands, Costa Rica, Dominica, Dominican Republic, El Salvador, Grenada, Guatemala, Haiti, Honduras, Jamaica, Montserrat, Netherlands Antilles, Panama, Saint Christopher-Nevis, Saint Lucia, Saint Vincent and the Grenadines, and Trinidad and Tobago.

4. See Arnade and Lee 1990 for an analysis of the covariance of nontraditional agricultural export prices, which they conclude is favorable to Central American producers. See Conroy et al. forthcoming for a similar analysis that draws a significantly different conclusion.

5. Trade statistics categorize processed nontraditional agricultural commodities, like canned juices and sauces, under industrial exports instead of agricultural exports, thus giving a somewhat exaggerated picture of the importance of the industrial sector. The vast majority of nontraditional exports are based on either agriculture or natural resources.

6. See Carroll et al. 1990 for a discussion of the pest-control dimensions of biodiversity and multiculture agroecosystems.

7. Pesticide imports can be a misleading indicator of pesticide use. In Guatemala, considerable amounts of chemicals were imported to formulate pesticide products exported to other parts of Latin America (Campos 1986). In Nicaragua, pesticides were purchased under favorable credit arrangements and then stockpiled for future use. Nevertheless, such data are useful indicators of general, long-term tendencies in pesticide use.

8. It is again important to recognize that pesticide illness rates declined in the

latter part of the 1980s with the decline of cotton. Thus the 1989 illness rate in León is probably lower than the rate of a decade earlier.

CHAPTER 5: PESTICIDES AND SOCIAL INEQUITY IN NONTRADITIONAL AGRICULTURE

1. Virtually all the violations involved the presence of chemicals for which no EPA tolerance existed. In 1987 only two of the fifty-two violations involved residues in excess of tolerances. Both cases involved the insecticide methamidophos on peppers.

2. The FDA can choose to place either individual exporters or all exporters of a given crop on automatic detention (also known as certification status). A certificate from a laboratory showing that tests were completed and no illegal pesticide residues were found on the produce must accompany all shipments. Cropwide automatic detention has the most severe implications for the largest number of growers, since all exporters and growers must incur the expenses and frequent sampling delays.

3. The wide range in the estimated losses is due partially to the poor quality of Dominican economic data (GAO 1986), as well as to the common practice of underinvoicing of export shipments to avoid Dominican taxes and facilitate capital flight, which results in an underestimation of economic activities.

4. These latter percentages are also relatively low, which may be because both surveys were taken in agricultural zones where pesticide use is common.

5. Simón et al. (1990) argue that pesticide application rates should be calculated from the number of doses applied rather than the number of applications. Traditionally, calculations have been based on the number of field applications, during which several chemicals may be applied in a mixture. The authors argue that the traditional method significantly understates the economic and ecological significance of application rates. In their method, an application containing two different products would count as two doses—a more precise representation of pesticide use than one application. In the case of Crehsul's application schedule, the alternative method would have counted twenty-seven doses instead of eleven applications.

6. See Barham et al. 1992 for a discussion of USAID's motivations for providing assistance to nontraditional agriculture in Guatemala. See Chapter 7 for details of USAID's and the chemical industry's projects in Guatemala.

7. See Krueger 1989 for a similar account of Joyabaj (southern El Quiché province) broccoli farmers driven to the brink of bankruptcy by market and exporter forces. To pay off loans for irrigation and other inputs necessary to enter into nontraditional farming, small farmers must migrate to the coast seasonally, selling their labor to the large plantations. See also Conroy et al. forthcoming.

8. The contribution of nontraditional agriculture to social and economic inequity is explored in greater detail in Conroy et al. forthcoming.

9. It's important to note that transnational mobility in response to ecological crisis is not a new phenomenon. The banana companies employed simi-

lar strategies decades earlier in Latin America to deal with plant diseases, as well as labor, international market, and other problems. See Brockett 1988:32.

10. The model from which these calculations were made was based on a farm size of ten hectares. Market prices, inputs and related economic variables were taken from 1985–1986 sources. Consequently, some calculations will change significantly in different years. For example, sesame prices have risen markedly since 1985, reducing, among other factors, the estimated time for recovery of investment. Sesame is now an appealing crop for small and medium-sized producers, and many former and current melon producers are entering into sesame farming. How long these favorable conditions will remain in effect is unknown.

11. Stanford (1991) discusses the political and economic dimensions of melon production in Apatzingán, another Mexican melon-producing region in crisis. See Wright 1990 for an extensive analysis of general pesticide problems in Mexican agriculture.

12. Transnational mobility also plagues the nontraditional industrial sector. Companies have reportedly abandoned free-trade zones in the Caribbean Basin after the tax breaks and other incentives, offered to lure these companies to the developing world, have expired. See McAfee 1991.

CHAPTER 6: THE SEARCH FOR SOLUTIONS:
INTEGRATED PEST MANAGEMENT

1. See in particular Farvar and Milton 1972 for early discussions on IPM in Third World settings.

2. See Conroy 1990 for a discussion of international assistance to Nicaragua during the Sandinista era.

3. See Murray 1984 for a more detailed discussion of this process.

4. This recognition has grown in part out of the successful experience of the FAO with farmer-based IPM efforts in Southeast Asian rice production. See FAO 1988, Hansen 1987, and Useem et al. 1992.

5. See Andrews et al. 1992 for a recent discussion of this question in Central America. See also Wilken 1987 and Chambers et al. 1990 for some of the classic statements of this perspective. This issue is the subject of a research project I am currently conducting with IPM specialist Peter Rosset, funded by the John D. and Catherine T. MacArthur Foundation, Program on Peace and International Cooperation.

6. For a more complete analysis of USAID's development strategy based on nontraditional exports and the related strategy to reduce basic grain production in Central America, see Conroy et al. forthcoming.

7. See Bentley 1989 for further work being carried out through Zamorano on producer-led technology development.

8. I am paraphrasing here the argument made by a high-level official for the National Agricultural Chemical Association in response to the talk I gave on pesticide problems in Central America at the U.S. Department of State.

This view remains a common one among agricultural technicians and, unfortunately, development planners and practitioners in the region as well.

CHAPTER 7: THE SEARCH FOR SOLUTIONS: THE SAFE-USE PARADIGM

1. See Keifer 1991 for an interesting preliminary analysis of the reduction in pesticide-related health problems on cooperatives participating in CARE IPM efforts in León, Nicaragua, as compared to nonparticipating cooperatives.
2. For a detailed discussion of the phenomenon of "blaming the victim," see Berman 1978.
3. Chemical company representatives denied any culpability in this epidemic and also questioned whether it even occurred. See Senate 1991 for company testimony and the responses of myself and several others who investigated the poisoning epidemic.
4. Wright 1990 provides similar evidence from Mexico.

CHAPTER 8: PESTICIDES, DEVELOPMENT, AND CRISIS: TOWARD A RESOLUTION

1. There are, of course, many more examples of alternatives than have been discussed in this book, some of which have been quite successful. See Chambers et al. 1990 and Hansen 1987.
2. See Sayer and Walker 1992 for an interesting analysis of this process in the global industrial sector.
3. Sweden, Norway, Holland, and Denmark have been increasingly important funders of environmental projects and organizations in the developing world. See DANIDA 1992 and Persson et al. 1991 for recent policy statements on Nordic commitments to environmental problems in Central America. Note that efforts to resolve pesticide problems, particularly through alternative agricultural measures, are priorities for funding from Nordic countries.
4. See Benton 1989 for an interesting discussion of assumptions concerning unlimited or renewable resources in Marxist theories of capitalist development.

Bibliography

Aglietta, Michel. 1979. *A theory of capitalist regulation*. London: New Left Books.

Agrichemical Age. 1989. Walter Cronkite loves you, but he's shy. *Agrichemical Age:* 14–16.

Alberti, Amalia M. 1991. *Impact of participation in non-traditional agricultural export production on the employment, income, and quality of life of women in Guatemala, Honduras, and Costa Rica*. Washington, D.C.: Chemonics. Contract AID 596-0108-C-00-6060-00.

Altieri, Miguel A., and Andres Yurjevic. 1989. The Latin American consortium on agroecology and development. *Development Anthropology Network* 7 (1): 17–19.

Andrews, Keith L., Jeffery W. Bentley, and Ronald D. Cave. 1992. Enhancing biological control's contribution to integrated pest management through appropriate levels of farmer participation. *Florida Entomologist* 75 (4): 429–439.

Annis, Sheldon. 1992. Evolving connectedness among environmental groups and grassroots organizations in protected areas of Central America. *World Development* 20 (4): 587–596.

Appel, Judith, Flor de Maria Matus, Inge Maria Beck, Tania García, Otilio Gonzales, and Jurrie Reiding. 1991. *Uso, manejo y riesgos asociados a plaguicidas en Nicaragua*. Managua: Confederación Universitaria Centroamericana.

Arnade, Carlos, and David Lee. 1990. *Risk aversion through nontraditional export promotion programs in Central America*. Agriculture and Trade Analysis Division, Economic Research Service, U.S. Department of Agriculture staff report AGES 9074.

Avery, Dennis T. 1985. Central America: Agriculture, technology, and unrest. *United States Department of State Intelligence Bulletin* 85 (2094): 70–73.

Barducci, Teodoro Boza. 1972. Ecological consequences of pesticides used for control of cotton insects in Cañete Valley, Peru. In *The careless technology: Ecology and international development*, ed. M. Taghi Farvar and John P. Milton, pp. 423–438. Garden City, N.Y.: Natural History Press.

Barham, Bradford, Mary Clark, Elizabeth Katz, and Rachel Schurman. 1992.

Nontraditional agricultural exports in Latin America. *Latin American Research Review* 27 (2): 43–82.

Barletta, Hector, and Alfredo Rueda. 1991. MIP en melones de exportación. *Agricultura de las Americas* Nov.–Dec.: 22–27.

Barry, Tom. 1987. *Roots of rebellion: Land and hunger in Central America.* Boston: South End Press.

Bentley, Jeffery W. 1989. What farmers don't know can't help them: The strengths and weaknesses of indigenous technical knowledge in Honduras. *Agriculture and Human Values* 6 (3): 25–31.

Bentley, Jeffery W., and Keith L. Andrews. 1991. Pests, peasants, and publications: Anthropological and entomological views of an integrated pest management program for small-scale Honduran farmers. *Human Organization* 50 (2): 113–124.

Benton, Ted. 1989. Marxism and natural limits: An ecological critique and reconstruction. *New Left Review* 178: 51–86.

Berman, Daniel M. 1978. *Death on the job: Occupational health and safety struggles in the United States.* New York: Monthly Review Press.

Blodgett, John E. 1974. Pesticides: Regulation of an evolving technology. In *Consumer health and product hazards/Cosmetics and drugs, pesticides, food additives,* ed. Samuel S. Epstein and Richard D. Grundy, Vol. 2, pp. 197–288. Cambridge, Mass.: MIT Press.

Boardman, Robert. 1986. *Pesticides in world agriculture: The politics of international regulation.* London: Macmillan Press.

Booth, John A., and Thomas Walker. 1989. *Understanding Central America.* Boulder, Colo.: Westview Press.

Brittin, W. A. 1950. Chemical agents in food. *Food, Drug, and Cosmetic Law Journal* 5 (Sept.): 590–597.

Brockett, Charles D. 1988. *Land, power, and poverty: Agrarian transformation and political conflict in Central America.* Boston: Unwin Hyman.

Bueso, José Antonio, Catherine Casteñeda, Flora Duarte, and Miriam O. Chavez. 1987. *Efectos de plaguicidas en Honduras.* Tegucigalpa: Universidad Nacional Autonoma de Honduras.

Bull, David. 1982. *A growing problem: Pesticides and the third world poor.* Oxford: OXFAM.

Bulmer-Thomas, Victor. 1987. *The political economy of Central America since 1920.* Cambridge: Cambridge University Press.

Byrnes, Kerry J. 1989. From melon patch to market place: How they learned to export a non-traditional crop. In In *AID/LAC/CDIE trade and investment workshop.* Alexandria, Va.: USAID.

Calderon, G. R., A. M. B. de Calderon, S. V. de Balcaceres, and A. J. de Maceda. 1981. *Residuos de lindano, dieldrina y DDT en suero de personas de diferentes zonas de El Salvador.* San Andres: Centro Nacional de Tecnología Agropecuaria.

Campos, Marit de. 1986. Problemas asociados con el uso de plaguicidas en Guatemala. Paper presented at Seminario sobre los problemas asociados con el uso de plaguicidas en Centroamerica y Panama in San José, Costa Rica.

Carroll, H. R., J. H. Vandermeer, and P. M. Rosset, ed. 1990. *Agroecology.* New York: McGraw Hill.

Castillo, Edvardo María. 1988. *Proyecto de ordenamiento del sistema productivo.* Managua: Ministerio de Desarrollo Agropecuario y Reforma Agraria.

Chambers, Robert, Arnold Pacey, and Lori Ann Thrupp. 1990. *Farmer first: Farmer innovation and agricultural research.* London: Intermediate Technology Publications.

Chapin, Georgeanne, and Robert Wasserstrom. 1983. Pesticide use and malaria resurgence in Central America and India. *Ecologist* 13 (4): 115–126.

CICP. 1988. *Environmental assessment of the Highlands agricultural development project.* College Park, Md.: Consortium for International Crop Protection. AID 520-0274.

Clark, W. A. Graham. 1909. *Cotton goods in Latin America.* Vol. 1, Cuba, Mexico, and Central America. Washington, D.C.: Department of Commerce and Labor, Bureau of Manufactures.

Cleaver, Harry. 1974. The origins of the green revolution. Dissertation, Stanford University.

Clyde, David F. 1987. Recent trends in epidemiology and the control of malaria. *Epidemiology Review* 9: 219.

CNPMPJD. 1991. *Folleto de analisis: Primer Congreso Nacional Campesino.* San José, Costa Rica: Consejo Nacional de Pequeños y Medianos Productores Justicia y Desarrollo.

Colburn, Forrest D. 1986. *Post-revolutionary Nicaragua: State, class, and the dilemmas of agrarian society.* Berkeley: University of California Press.

Cole, Donald C., Rob McConnell, Douglas L. Murray, and Feliciano Pacheco Anton. 1988. Pesticide illness surveillance: The Nicaraguan experience. *Bulletin of the Pan American Health Organization* 22 (2): 119–132.

Conroy, Michael E. 1989. *The diversification of Central American exports: Chimera or reality?* Atlanta: Latin American Studies Association Congress.

———. 1990. The political economy of the 1990 Nicaraguan elections. *International Journal of Political Economy* 20(3):5–33.

Conroy, Michael T., Douglas L. Murray, and Peter Rosset. Forthcoming. *The fruits of crisis in Central America: Gambling on nontraditional agriculture.*

Conservation Foundation. 1988. *Opportunities to assist developing countries in the proper use of agricultural and industrial chemicals.* Washington, D.C.: Committee on Health and Environment and the Conservation Foundation.

Contreras, Mario. 1990. *Situation, perspective, and strategies for the use of pesticides in Central America.* Guatemala: Regional Office for Central American Programs, USAID/Guatemala.

DANIDA. 1992. *Environmental sector support: Strategic framework, control of pesticide use, Central America, First Draft.* Copenhagen: Danish International Development Agency.

Daxl, Rainer, Sean Swezey, Carlos Marin, and Ivan Gallo. 1990. La supresion del picudo, *Anthonomous grandis* Boh. (Coleopt: Curculionidae) en intertemporada algodónera en Nicaragua, 1981–1984. Paper presented at Cuarto Congreso Nacional MIP/Tercero Congreso Internacional in Managua, Nicaragua.

De Janvry, Alain. 1981. *The agrarian question and reformism in Latin America.* Baltimore: Johns Hopkins University Press.

Dinham, Barbara. 1991. FAO and pesticides: Promotion or proscription? *Ecologist* 21 (2):61–65.

Domhoff, G. William. 1978. *The powers that be: Processes of ruling class domination in America.* New York: Random House.

Dosal, Paul J. 1985. Accelerating dependent development and revolution: Nicaragua and the alliance for progress. *Environmental Law Quarterly* 38 (3): 75–96.

Dunlap, Thomas R. 1981. *DDT: Scientists, citizens, and public policy.* Princeton: Princeton University Press.

Edwards, C. A. 1986. Agrochemicals as environmental pollutants. In *Control of pesticide applications and residues in food: A guide and directory,* ed. B. von Hofsten and G. Ekstrom, pp. 1–19. Uppsala: Swedish Science Press.

Ehrlich, Paul. 1992. Morrison Institute for Population Studies lecture, Stanford University, January 8.

Ekins, Paul. 1992. *A new world order: Grassroots movements for global change.* New York: Routledge, Chapman and Hall.

Enriquez, Laura. 1991. *Harvesting change.* Chapel Hill: University of North Carolina Press.

Epstein, Samuel S. 1979. *The politics of cancer.* New York: Anchor Books.

Escobar, Arturo. 1988. Power and visibility: Development and the invention and management of the Third World. *Cultural Anthropology* 3 (4): 428–443.

———. 1992. Imagining a post-development era? Critical thought, development, and social movements. *Social Text* (31–32):20–56.

Faber, Daniel. 1991. A sea of poison. *Report on the Americas* 25 (2):31–36.

———. 1993. *Environment under fire: Imperialism and the ecological crisis in Central America.* New York: Monthly Review Press.

Fagen, Richard. 1987. *Forging peace: The challenge of Central America.* New York: Basil Blackwell.

Falcon, L. A., and R. Daxl. 1977. *Informe al gobierno de Nicaragua sobre control integrado de plagas del algodonero.* Managua: Food and Agriculture Organization, United Nations Development Program.

Falcon, L. A., and R. Smith. 1973. *Guidelines for integrated control of* cotton pests. Rome: Food and Agriculture Organization of the United Nations.

FAO. 1980. *Control integrado de plagas agricolas, Nicaragua: Resultados y recomendaciones del proyecto.* Rome: Food and Agriculture Organization of the United Nations.

———. 1984. *Integrated pest control in agriculture: Report of the twelfth session of the FAO/UNEP Panel of Experts meeting.* Rome: Food and Agriculture Organization of the United Nations.

———. 1988. *Integrated pest control in agriculture: Report of the thirteenth session of the FAO/UNEP Panel of Experts meeting, Rome, 22–24 September, 1987.* Food and Agriculture Organization of the United Nations.

———. 1990a. *Centroamerica: Estudio regional del algodón.* Food and Agriculture Organization of the United Nations.

———. 1990b. Annex 2. In *Centroamerica: Estudio regional del algodón.* Food and Agriculture Organization of the United Nations.

———. 1992. FAO biennial conference report. *Global Pesticide Monitor* 2(1):7.

Farm and Chemical Handbook. 1992. Willoughby, Ohio: Meister Publishing Co.

Farvar, M. Taghi, and John P. Milton, ed. 1972. *The careless technology: Ecology and international development.* Garden City, N.Y.: Natural History Press.

FDA. 1989. *World wide import detention summary (Fiscal Year 1989).* Washington, D.C.: Department of Health and Human Services, Food and Drug Administration.

Fogel, Robert W., and Stanley L. Engerman. 1974. *Time on the cross: The economics of American Negro slavery.* Vol. 1. Boston: Little, Brown.

Foundation for Advancements in Science and Education. 1993. Exporting banned and hazardous pesticides, 1991 statistics. *FASE Reports* 2 (1): S1–S8.

Freeman, David M. 1989. *Local organizations for social development: Concepts and cases of irrigation organization.* Boulder, Colo.: Westview Press.

GAO. 1986. *Caribbean Basin Initiative: Need for more reliable data on business activity resulting from the initiative.* Washington, D.C.: U.S. General Accounting Office.

Glover, D., and K. Kusterer. 1990. *Small farmers, big business: Contract farming and rural development.* New York: St. Martin's Press.

Gorostiaga, Xabier, and Peter Marchetti. 1988. The Central American economy: Conflict and crisis. In *Crisis in Central America: Regional dynamics and U.S. policy in the 1980s*, ed. Nora Hamilton, Jeffry A. Frieden, Linda Fuller, and Manuel Pastor Jr. Boulder, Colo.: Westview Press.

Guerra-Borges, Alfredo. 1989. Industrial development in Central America,

1960–1980: Issues in debate. In *Central America: Regional dynamics and U.S. policy in the 1980s,* ed. George Holland and Stuart Irvin. Boulder, Colo.: Westview Press.

Hansen, Michael. 1987. *Escape from the pesticide treadmill: Alternatives to pesticides in developing countries.* Mount Vernon, N.Y.: Institute for Consumer Policy Research.

———. 1990. *The first three years: Implementation of the World Bank pesticide guidelines, 1985–1988.* Washington, D.C.: Consumer Policy Institute, Consumers Union.

Harman, John W. 1990. *Five Latin American countries' controls over the registration and use of pesticides.* Testimony submitted to the Committee on Agriculture, Nutrition, and Forestry, United States Senate. Government Accounting Office/T-RECD-90-57.

Hayes, Wayland J. 1982. *Pesticides studied in man.* Baltimore: Williams and Wilkins.

Hayes, W. J., and E. R. Lawes, ed. 1991. *Handbook of pesticide toxicology.* San Diego: Academic Press.

Holl, Karen, Gretchen Daily, and Paul R. Ehrlich. 1990. Integrated pest management in Latin America. *Environmental Conservation* 17 (4): 341–350.

Hooper, Kim. 1982. *Cancer risk assessment and proposed urine monitoring program for chlordimeform.* Berkeley: California Department of Health Services. Memorandum.

Hoppin, Polly. 1989. *Pesticide use in four non-traditional crops in Guatemala: Implications for residues.* College Park, Md.: Consortium for International Crop Protection.

———. 1991. Pesticide use on four non-traditional crops in Guatemala: Program and policy implications. Doctoral dissertation, Johns Hopkins University.

Huntington, Samuel P. 1968. *Political order in changing societies.* New Haven: Yale University Press.

ICAITI. 1977. *An environmental and economic study of the consequences of pesticide use in Central American cotton production.* Instituto Centroamericano de Investigación y Tecnología Industrial. UNEP 0205-73-002 and 0108-75-007.

Jennings, Bruce H. 1988. *Foundations of international agricultural research: Science and politics in Mexican agriculture.* Boulder, Colo.: Westview Press.

Jeyaratnam, J. 1990. Pesticide poisoning: A major global health problem. *World Health Statistics Quarterly* 43: 139–144.

Jones, Jacqueline. 1992. *The dispossessed: America's underclasses from the Civil War to the present.* New York: Basic Books.

Kahn, Ephraim. 1976. Pesticide-related illness in California farm workers. *Journal of Occupational Health* 18: 693–696.

Kaimowitz, David. 1992. Aid and development in Latin America. *Latin American Research Review* 27 (2): 202–211.

Keifer, Matthew C. 1991. *Protective effect on cholinesterase levels of an integrated pest management program in Nicaraguan basic grain farmers.* Managua: CARE International.

Keifer, Matthew C., and Feliciano Pacheco. 1991. *Reporte de encuesta de subregistro de intoxicaciones con plaguicidas sobre el año 1989, region 2, León, Nicaragua.* Managua: CARE International.

Kissinger, Henry, et al. 1984. *Report of the National Bipartisan Commission on Central America.* Washington, D.C.: U.S. Government Printing Office.

Klaassen, C., M. Amdur, and J. Doull, ed. 1986. *Casarett and Doull's toxicology: The basic science of poisons.* New York: Macmillan Publishing Co.

Kline, Willi. 1988. *Contaminación ambiental por organochlorados.* Managua: Centro Nacional de Hygiene y Epidemiología, Ministerio de Salud.

Knirsch, Jurgen. 1991. Pesticides in the global marketplace. *Global Pesticide Monitor* 1 (3): 1–7.

Korten, David C., and Felipe B. Alfonso, ed. 1983. *Bureaucracy and the poor: Closing the gap.* West Hartford, Conn.: Kumarian Press.

Krieger, R. I., P. P. Feeny, and C. F. Wilkinson. 1971. Detoxification enzymes in the guts of caterpillars: An evolutionary answer to plant defenses. *Science* 172:579–581.

Krueger, Chris. 1989. Development and politics in rural Guatemala. *Development Anthropology Network* 7 (1): 1–6.

Leonard, H. Jeffrey. 1987. *Natural resources and economic development in Central America: A regional environmental profile.* New Brunswick: Transaction Books.

Levine, R. S. 1985. *Informal consultation on planning strategy for the prevention of pesticide poisoning.* Geneva: World Health Organization. Unpublished document.

Lewis, C. F., and T. R. Richmond. 1968. Cotton as a crop. In *Advances in production and utilization of quality cotton: Principles and practices,* ed. F. C. Elliot, M. Hoover, and W. K. Porter. Ames: Iowa State University Press.

Lipset, Seymour, and Aldo Solari. 1967. *Elites in Latin America.* New York: Oxford University Press.

Lopez, José Gabriel. 1990. Agrarian transformation and the political, ideological, and cultural responses from the base: A case study from western Mexico. Doctoral dissertation, University of Texas, Austin.

Marenco, Roberto. 1990. *Informe preliminar de actividades del departmento de proteccion vegetal de la escuela agricola Panamericana en el programa de manejo integrado de plagas de cucurbitas en el sur de Honduras.* Zamorano, Honduras: Escuela Agricola Panamericana.

Marquardt, Sandra, and Laura Glassman. 1990. *Never-registered pesticides: Rejected toxics join the "circle of poison."* Washington, D.C.: Greenpeace.

Martorell, Reynaldo, and Haley Kaplowitz. 1990. Consequences of stunting in early childhood for adult body size in rural Guatemala. *Annales Nestle* 48:85–92.

Martorell, Reynaldo, Juan Rivera, Haley Kaplowitz, and Ernesto Pollitt. 1991. Long-term consequences of growth retardation during early childhood. Paper presented at Sixth International Congress of Auxology in Madrid.

Mathieson, John A. 1988. Dominican Republic. In *Struggle against dependency: Nontraditional export growth in Central America and the Caribbean*, ed. Eva Paus. Boulder, Colo.: Westview Press.

Mathiessen, Constance. 1992. The day the poison stopped working. *Mother Jones* March–April: 48–55.

McAfee, Kathy. 1991. *Storm signals: Structural adjustment and development alternatives in the Caribbean*. Boston: Oxfam America.

McCamant, John F. 1968. *Development assistance in Central America*. New York: Praeger.

McConnell, Rob. 1988. Epidemiology and occupational health in developing countries: Pesticides in Nicaragua. In *Progress in occupational epidemiology*, ed. C. Hogstedt and C. Reuterwall, pp. 361–365. Uppsala: Elsevier Science Publishers.

McConnell, Rob, Feliciano Pacheco, Nestor Castro, and Matthew Keifer. 1990. Poisoning epidemics and preventative health care. *Global Pesticide Monitor* 1 (2): 10–11.

McConnell, Rob, Feliciano Pacheco, and Douglas L. Murray. 1992. Hazards of closed pesticide mixing and loading systems: The paradox of protective technology in the Third World. *British Journal of Industrial Medicine* 49 (9): 615–620.

McConnell, Rob, Matthew Keifer, and Linda Rosenstock. 1993. Elevated tactile vibration threshold among workers previously poisoned with methamidophos. *American Journal of Industrial Medicine*, in press.

McConnell, Rob, Mario Cordon, and Douglas L. Murray. Submitted. Subclinical health effects of environmental pesticide contamination in a Third World setting: Cholinesterase depression in children. *Environmental Research*.

Mendes, Rene. 1977. *Informe sobre salud occupacional de trabajadores agrícolas en Centro America y Panama*. Washington, D.C.: Pan American Health Organization.

Milius, Peter, and Dan Morgan. 1976. Hazardous pesticides shipped abroad as aid. *Washington Post* December 8.

Mohs, Edgar. 1986. La orquesta Marxista internacional. *La Nación* December 25.

Molina, Gustavo. 1989. *Informe de viaje 460: San Pedro Sula y Tegucigalpa, Honduras*. Mexico City: Pan American Health Organization.

Mott, Lawrie, and Karen Snyder. 1988. *Pesticide alert: A guide to pesticides in fruits and vegetables*. New York: Sierra Books.

Murray, Douglas L. 1982. The abolition of El Cortito, the short-handled hoe:

A case study in social conflict and state policy in California agriculture. *Social Problems* 30 (1): 26–39.

———. 1984. Social problem-solving in a revolutionary setting: Nicaragua's pesticide policy reforms. *Policy Studies Review* 5 (2): 214–219.

———. 1989a. *Developing integrated pest management in the Dominican Republic.* IRI Research Institute.

———. 1989b. Pesticide problems and international nongovernmental organizations: The Nicaraguan experience. *Development Anthropology Network* 7 (1): 6–9.

———. 1991. Export agriculture, ecological disruption, and inequitable development: Some effects of pesticides in southern Honduras. *Agriculture and Human Values* 8 (4): 19–29.

Murray, Douglas L., Michael Giuliano, and S. Anwar Rizvi. 1989. *Dominican Republic: The agricultural exports protection report.* Washington, D.C.: Development Alternatives.

Murray, Douglas L., and Polly Hoppin. 1992. Recurring contradictions in agrarian development: Pesticide problems in Caribbean Basin nontraditional agriculture. *World Development* 20 (4): 597–608.

Murray, Douglas L., and Rob McConnell. 1987. *Pesticide problems among small farmers in Costa Rica: An evaluation and recommendations for CARE Costa Rica.* New York: CARE International.

NACA. 1981. *White paper: The IPM issue.* Washington, D.C.: North American Chemical Association.

National Academy of Sciences. 1989. *Alternative agriculture.* Washington, D.C.: NAS Press.

NEST. 1992. *Tierra viva, living earth: A program in sustainable agriculture and environmental education for El Salvador.* San Francisco: New El Salvador Today Foundation.

Nigh, Ronald. 1991. *Associative corporations, organic agriculture, and the new peasant movement in Mexico.* Mexico City: Centro de Ecología, Universidad Nacional Autónoma de Mexico. Draft.

Noe Pino, Hugo, and Rodulio Perdomo. 1991. *Impacto de las politicas de fomento a las exportaciones no tradicionales sobre pequeños y medianos productores: Caso del cultivo del melón y camarón.* Tegucigalpa, Honduras: Postagrado Centroamericano en Economía y Planificación del Desarrollo.

Paarlberg, Robert L. 1991. Managing pesticide use in developing countries: The limits of international cooperation. In *The effectiveness of international environmental institutions: Introduction and analytical framework,* ed. Peter M. Haas, Robert O. Keohane, and Marc A. Levy. Cambridge, Mass.: Center for International Affairs, Harvard University.

Pacheco, Feliciano A. 1987. *Resultados de las muestras de clordimeform (CDF) en Orina.* León: Ministerio de Salud, Dirección General de Higiene y Epidemiología.

Paige, Jeffrey M. 1985. Cotton and revolution in Nicaragua. In *State versus markets in the world-system*, ed. Peter Evans, Dietrich Rueschemeyer, and Evelyn Huber Stephens, pp. 91–114. Beverly Hills, Calif.: Sage Publications.

Pearse, Andrew. 1980. *Seeds of plenty, seeds of want: Social and economic implications of the green revolution*. New York: Oxford University Press.

Perkins, John H. 1980. The quest for innovation in agricultural entomology, 1945–1978. In *Pest control: Cultural and environmental aspects*, ed. David Pimentel and John H. Perkins, pp. 23–80. Boulder, Colo.: Westview Press.

———. 1982. *Insects, experts, and the insecticide crisis: The quest for new pest management strategies*. New York: Plenum Press.

Persson, Reidar, Jan Robberts, Pierre Fruhling, Soren Wium-Anderson, and Kari Silfverber. 1991. *Ecology for growth: Report from a Nordic mission on environment to Central America*. Swedish International Development Agency and Danish International Development Agency.

Pimentel, David, and Hugh Lehman, eds. 1993. *The pesticide question: Environment, economics, and ethics*. New York: Chapman Hill.

Raynolds, Laura. 1992. The restructuring of export agriculture in the Dominican Republic: Changing agrarian production relations and the state. Doctoral dissertation, Cornell University.

———. 1991. Export substitution and the rise of non-traditional agricultural commodities in the Dominican Republic. Paper presented at Sixteenth International Congress of the Latin American Studies Association in Washington, D.C.

Repetto, Robert. 1985. *Paying the price: Pesticide subsidies in developing countries*. Washington, D.C.: World Resources Institute.

Riding, Alan. 1980. Guatemala: State of siege. *New York Times Magazine* August 24.

Roldán, Carmen. 1991. *Evaluación preliminar del material impreso "Educación ambiental y agropecuaria." Guía didactica para el docente: Plaguicidas*. Herédia: Universidad de Costa Rica.

Rosenstock, Linda, Matthew Keifer, William E. Daniell, Rob McConnell, and Keith Claypoole. 1991. Chronic central nervous system effects of acute organophosphate pesticide intoxication. *Lancet* July 26.

Rosset, Peter M. 1987. Precios, subvenciones y los niveles de dano economico. *Manejo Integrado de Plagas (Costa Rica)* 6:27–35.

Rostow, Walt Whitman. 1960. *The stages of economic growth: A non-communist manifesto*. Cambridge: Cambridge University Press.

Sanford, Terry, et al. 1989. *The report of the international commission for Central American recovery and development: Poverty, conflict, and hope—A Turning point in Central America*. Durham, N.C.: Duke University Press.

Sayer, Andrew, and Richard Walker. 1992. *The new social economy: Reworking the division of labor*. Cambridge, Mass.: Blackwell Publishers.

Schneider, Keith. 1993. Environmentalists fight each other over trade accord. *New York Times* September 9.

Schulten, G. G. M. N.d. *Integrated pest management in developing countries.* Rome: FAO.

Science News Letter. 1945. DDT can wipe out plagues. September 8:149.

Senate, U.S. 1991. *Circle of poison: Impact on American consumer.* Committee on Agriculture, Nutrition, and Forestry, Senate hearing.

Sesmou, Khalil. 1991. The Food and Agriculture Organization of the United Nations: An insider's view. *Ecologist* 21 (2):47–56.

Simón, Jorge J., Rolando Martinez, Maritza Vargas, Mauro Paniagua, Nestor Jirón, Julio Bohorquez, and Peter Rosset. 1990. Diagnóstico de factores que incidieron en el rendimiento del algodón en el ciclo 89–90 en la region occidental de Nicaragua. Paper presented at Fourth National Congress for Integrated Pest Management, October 23–26, in Managua, Nicaragua.

Sinks, Alfred H. 1944. Another enemy surrenders. *Popular Science* June: 56A–D.

Smith, Ray F., and Harold T. Reynolds. 1972. Effects of manipulation of cotton agro-ecosystems on insect pest populations. In *The careless technology: Ecology and international development,* ed. M. Taghi Farvar and John P. Milton, pp. 373–438. Garden City, N.Y.: Natural History Press.

Stanford, Lois. 1991. Mexico's fresh fruit and vegetable export system: Recent developments and their impact on local economies. In *Fresh fruit and vegetables globalization network, in University of California, Santa Cruz.*

Stein, Stanley. 1957. *Brazilian cotton textile manufacture.* Cambridge, Mass.: Harvard University Press.

Stonich, Susan C. 1993. I am destroying the land: The political ecology of poverty and environmental destruction in Honduras. Boulder, Colo.: Westview Press.

Stonich, Susan C., Douglas L. Murray, and Peter M. Rosset. 1992. Enduring crises: The human and environmental consequences of nontraditional export growth in Central America. Paper presented at Ninety-first Annual meeting of the American Anthropological Association, December 2–7, 1992, in San Francisco.

Swezey, Sean, and Daniel Faber. 1988. Disarticulated accumulation, agroexport, and ecological crisis in Nicaragua: The case of cotton. *Capitalism, Nature, Socialism* 1 (1):47–68.

Swezey, Sean L., and M. L. Salamanca. 1987. Susceptibility of the boll weevil (Coleoptera: Curulionidae) to methyl parathion in Nicaragua. *Journal of Economic Entomology* 80:358–361.

Swezey, Sean L., Douglas L. Murray, and Rainer G. Daxl. 1986. Nicaragua's revolution in pesticide policy. *Environment* 28 (1): 6–9, 29–36.

Tabora, Panfilo. 1990. *Evaluación de veinticinco cultivos con perspectivas en Honduras.* La Lima: Fundación Hondureña de Investigación Agrícola.

Thrupp, Lori Ann. 1988. The political ecology of pesticide use in developing countries: Dilemmas in the banana sector of Costa Rica. Ph.D. dissertation, University of Sussex.

Trivelato, Maria D., and Catharina Wesseling. 1991. *El uso de los plaguicidas en Costa Rica y sus consecuencias.* Herédia: Universidad Nacional de Costa Rica.

UNDP. 1991. *Human development report 1991.* United Nations Development Program. New York: Oxford University Press.

Universidad del Valle. 1993. *Impacto de cultivos horticolas no-tradicionales de exportación sobre plagas, organismos beneficos y suelo en el altiplano de Guatemala.* Universidad del Valle de Guatemala, Instituto de Investigaciones.

USAID. 1990. *Agricultural sector strategy paper.* Tegucigalpa: Office of Agricultural and Rural Development, United States Agency for International Development, Honduras.

USCG. 1990. *Cambios económicos producidos por la expansion de la horticultura de exportación en la organización social de las configuraciones socioculturales de Patzicía y Zaragoza, Chimaltenango.* San Carlos: Escuela de Historia, Universidad de San Carlos de Guatemala.

Useem, Michael, Louis Setti, and Jonathan Pincus. 1992. The science of Javanese management: Organizational alignment in an Indonesian development programme. *Public Administration and Development* 12: 447–471.

Van den Bosch, Robert. 1980. *The pesticide conspiracy.* New York: Anchor Books.

Vaughn, M., and G. Leon. 1977. Pesticide management in a major crop with severe resistance problems. In *Fifteenth International Congress of Entomology, in Washington, D.C.*, pp. 812–815.

Villagran, E. 1981. An evaluation of integrated pest control efforts in Central America and a management strategy to optimize future programs. In *Tenth session of the FAO UNEP panel of experts on integrated pest control, in Rome.*

VonBraun, Joachim, David Hotchkiss, and Maarten Immink. 1989. *Nontraditional export crops in Guatemala: Effects on production, income, and nutrition.* Report 73. Washington, D.C.: International Food Policy Research Institute.

Vunderink, Gregg L. 1989. *Peasant participation and mobilization during economic crisis: The case of Costa Rica.* Texas Papers on Latin America 89-14. Austin: Institute of Latin American Studies, University of Texas.

Walker, Dana. 1992. Ethnic and national cultures of resistance: The Subtiavan Indians in Nicaraguan history. Master's thesis, University of Texas, Austin.

Walker, Thomas W. 1991. *Nicaragua: The land of Sandino.* 3d ed. Boulder, Colo.: Westview Press.

Warner, Rose Ella, and C. Earle Smith. 1968. Boll weevil found in pre-Columbian cotton from Mexico. *Science* 162:911–912.

Weinger, Merri, and Mark Lyons. 1992. Problem-solving in the fields: An action-oriented approach to farmworker education about pesticides. *American Journal of Industrial Medicine* 22(5):677.

Weir, David, and Mark Shapiro. 1981. *Circle of poison: Pesticides and people in a hungry world.* San Francisco: Institute for Food and Development Policy.

WHO. 1973. *Safe use of pesticides.* Technical Report Series 513. Geneva: World Health Organization.

———. 1989. *Public health impact of pesticides used in agriculture.* Geneva: World Health Organization.

Wilken, Gene C. 1987. *Good farmers: Traditional agricultural resource management in Mexico and Central America.* Berkeley: University of California Press.

Williams, Robert G. 1986. *Export agriculture and the crisis in Central America.* Chapel Hill: University of North Carolina Press.

Wolf, Eric R. 1982. *Europe and the people without history.* Berkeley: University of California Press.

Wolff, Mary S., Paolo G. Toniolo, Eric W. Lee, Marilyn Rivera, and Neil Dubin. 1993. Blood levels of organochlorine residues and risk of breast cancer. *Journal of the National Cancer Institute* 85 (8):648–652.

Wolterding, Martin. 1981. The poisoning of Central America. *Sierra* (Sept.–Oct.).

Wright, Angus. 1990. *The death of Ramon Gonzalez: The modern agricultural dilemma.* Austin: University of Texas Press.

Zind, Tom. 1990. Pretto lures U.S. melon business. *Packer* March 10.

Zuvekas, Clarence. 1992. Alternative perspectives on Central American economic recovery and development. *Latin American Research Review* 27 (1):125–150.

Index